ORIGIN PROBLEM SOLVING
THE LEAN APPROACH TO COMPLEX PROBLEMS

ORIGIN PROBLEM SOLVING
THE LEAN APPROACH TO COMPLEX PROBLEMS

Dustin Thomas

Origin Problem Solving

First Edition, 2024

Copyright © 2024 by Dustin Thomas

All rights reserved. No part of this publication may be reproduced, distributed, or transmitted in any form or by any means, including photocopying, recording, or other electronic or mechanical methods, without the prior written permission of the publisher, except in the case of brief quotations embodied in critical articles and reviews.

Published by Dustin Thomas

3828 Thorncrest Dr

Jackson, MI 49203

OriginProblemSolving@Outlook.com

https://www.youtube.com/@ORIGINproblemsolving

ISBN: 9798329202083

The author does not provide professional advice or services to individual readers. The ideas, procedures, and suggestions presented in this book are not intended to replace the guidance of competent legal counsel from an attorney licensed to practice in your jurisdiction. The author assumes no liability or responsibility for any loss or damage allegedly resulting from the use of the information or suggestions contained in this book.

Title: Origin Problem Solving / Dustin Thomas.

Editing by Melissa Sherman

Printed in United States of America

DEDICATION

To God, for His grace and inspiration, and to my family, whose unwavering love and support are my constant source of strength.

CONTENTS

Introduction

Chapter 1: Continuous Improvement Culture

Chapter 2: Stories of Success and Failure

Chapter 3: Lean 8 Steps of Problem Solving

Chapter 4: Step 0 – Preparation

Chapter 5: Step 1 – Perception

Chapter 6: Step 2 – Define our Problem

Chapter 7: Step 3 – Break Down our Problem

Chapter 8: Step 4 – Identify and Locate

Chapter 9: Step 5 - Analyze the Root Cause

Chapter 10: Step 6 – Take Action

Chapter 11: Step 7 - Monitor for Effectiveness

Chapter 12: Step 8 - Standardize Success

Final Thoughts

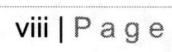

INTRODUCTION
ORIGIN PROBLEM SOLVING

Today's intricate world demands the ability to navigate problems of various complexities and environments. However, many individuals and organizations are stuck in a traditional line of thinking and are trapped within processes that are anything but efficient. The Lean approach is a methodology that began on the floors of Toyota's manufacturing plants but has quickly become much bigger than that, providing a powerful culture for solving the wide-ranging problems that are faced in the modern world.

The Lean methodology combines principles of continuous improvement, investment in people, and a relentless pursuit of waste elimination. It is a culture of collaboration and learning, and this book underscores how the Lean methodology, which runs on empowerment and efficiency, is best suited for tackling the problems faced in a complex world. Solving these problems requires that we stop letting our traditional mindsets hold us back from learning, collaborating and innovating. We must look beyond heroism and top-down problem solving.

This frequently used tactic sometimes momentarily relieves the symptoms but almost always produces a complex process of work arounds and pain points, just to have the same issues return. We must instead build a mindset that can greatly change the culture of your organization, putting people first and enlisting them to improve upon their processes. It is my aspiration that this book will aid you in creating a new culture centered on continuous improvement.

As you read Origin Problem Solving, I'll take you through the Lean approach and teach you how it can relate to problems as well as the people trying to solve them. I will explore actual examples of its practices and take you through specific steps that you can take right now to help bring Lean into your problem-solving culture.

> *We must look beyond heroism and top-down problem solving.*

I don't want to just teach you the tools of Lean. I candidly share the full, complete and honest picture of Lean including the mistakes. It was astonishing to discover that Lean could be used not only to solve problems but also to create a collaborative environment where everyone felt empowered to contribute to something meaningful and beneficial for all. My hope is that through these lessons and these steps that you too can see how to shift your own organization or team towards Lean problem solving. Readers can expect various Lean principles embedded into the book that once I understood them, helped me confidently grow and lead a culture that truly empowered people to undertake seemingly impossible things. Whether you're seasoned in Lean or a newcomer, I hope this book helps you make a giant leap forward in adopting Lean as a way of thinking for yourself and your organization and you find things that help you solve your problems.

Once you've finished reading this book, you will have the tools and mindset needed to approach complicated problems with confidence and you'll be able to create a culture that celebrates continuous improvement and solving problems together.

Waste Elimination

Many years ago, while several years into my first Lean rollout, a critical event reshaped my grasp of Lean principles, particularly in recognizing and eliminating waste. After years of internal assessments and cross-functional reviews to gauge our progress with Lean, we enlisted an external contractor to offer a fresh perspective. This external review stirred significant anxiety among the management team, as it tested not only our operational practices but also our leadership of Lean principles.

One day, while I was discussing operations in the supervisor's office, a man abruptly entered and asked if I was the Production Manager. Upon confirming, he immediately challenged my knowledge of the eight forms of waste. Caught off guard, I faltered, unable to provide a clear response. His direct follow-up questioned how he could trust my ability to identify waste during our Gemba walks if I couldn't name the types of wastes we aimed to eliminate. At the time, I was not familiar with the DOWNTIME acronym, which encapsulates the eight forms of waste:

1. **Defects:** These are flaws or errors in a product or service that require additional time, resources, and expenditure to rectify. Defects often lead to rework or scrapping of products, impacting both cost efficiency and customer satisfaction.

2. **Overproduction:** This occurs when more products are produced than are immediately needed by customers. This includes internal customers such as multiple files of the same content or memos and emails to everyone.

3. **Waiting:** This type of waste is characterized by idle time when resources are not being used effectively. Waiting occurs between processes or activities, often due to bottlenecks, poor workflow alignment, or inefficient scheduling, leading to delays and reduced productivity.

4. **Non-utilized Talent:** Often overlooked, this waste occurs when the skills, knowledge, and abilities of employees are not fully utilized. Whether it's through under-challenging assignments or a lack of empowerment, failing to leverage existing talent can stifle innovation and employee satisfaction.

5. **Transportation:** Unnecessary movement of materials, products, or information between processes adds no value and increases the risk of damage, delays, and costs.

6. **Inventory:** Excess inventory involves holding more supplies, materials, or products than what is needed for immediate production or demand.

7. **Motion Waste:** This refers to any unnecessary movement by people within their work environment. These movements do not add value to the product or service and often include actions such as reaching, bending, or walking excessive distances.

8. **Excess Processing:** This type of waste occurs when more work or a higher quality level is performed than is required by the customer. This may look like excess approvals and signatures or long extended unproductive meetings.

This experience was a pivotal learning moment, teaching me the critical need to deeply understand and articulate Lean principles effectively. It wasn't just about compliance but about genuinely enhancing and transforming our operations. If I wasn't fully aware of all the forms of waste, how would I expect my Team to be fully aware?

With that I want to ensure you read and study the 8 forms of waste. When doing so, it's common for questions to arise about whether a particular issue is "Transportation or Motion" or "Excess Processing or Overproduction" or "this waste or that waste." While there are correct answers to these questions, the distinction becomes moot once the waste is identified. My advice is to focus on understanding the eight forms of waste thoroughly. If you happen to categorize a specific waste incorrectly, don't dwell on it too much; the crucial step is that you've recognized the presence of waste, and even more is what are YOU going to do about it.

CHAPTER 1
CONTINUOUS IMPROVEMENT CULTURE

At the heart of Lean methodology lies the principle of continuous improvement, a relentless pursuit of perfection through incremental changes which is referred to at times as 'Kaizen'. This principle is not just about optimizing processes but, in this journey, I have found it to be deeply rooted in respect for people. It's the belief that those doing the work have the most valuable insights into how it can be

Problems should be addressed not from a distant managerial perspective but from the ground up, with the insights and experiences of those who face them daily.

improved. Continuous improvement is a mindset, a culture that sees every problem as an opportunity for growth and learning.

Empowering

The essence of solving problems effectively within a Lean framework is to involve those who are directly engaged with the work. Problems should be addressed not from a distant managerial perspective but from the ground up, with the insights and experiences of those who face them daily. This approach not only leverages intimate knowledge of the work but also fosters a sense of ownership and engagement among employees. We should be empowering our employees to make decisions and take action. In addition, we also need to ensure that we are recognizing and valuing contributions. Acknowledging workers' expertise in their processes and their daily work, while respecting their insights and contributions is not only what is deserved but it is what is *needed* to achieve performance. In addition, we need to nurture a collaborative and supportive culture where respect for people is paramount. This results in a deliberate and sustained effort from everyone involved to ensure individuals feel valued and empowered to contribute. This is not only for our coworkers but also a benefit of effective problem solving, innovation, and overall performance.

Leadership's Role

Leadership in a Lean environment undergoes a transformative shift from traditional command-and-control to a more facilitative and coaching role. Leaders are enablers of continuous improvement, providing the necessary resources, training, and most importantly, the time for their teams to engage in problem-solving activities. They create an environment where experimentation is encouraged, and failures are seen as steppingstones to knowledge and improvement. Leaders support their teams in problem-solving and improvement efforts, providing guidance while respecting their autonomy and expertise.

Practical Problem Solving

Practical Problem Solving in the context of Lean is a systematic approach that empowers individuals and teams to address challenges directly, efficiently, and effectively. This section will outline key steps in the Problem-Solving process and highlight how a structured approach can facilitate problem resolution.

Key Steps in Practical Problem Solving:

0. Preparation: Important in Kaizen events, having the data and a plan of attack ready so when the larger group gets together, we can execute efficiently and effectively. This is also where Short-Term countermeasures are deployed.

1. Perception: Aligning on what we are problem solving to get everyone on the same page.

2. Define Our Problem: Setting our Target, Actual, and Gap.

3. Break Down Our Problem: Taking a whole pie of a problem and breaking it down into easier to tackle slices.

4. Identify and Locate: SMART TARGET and Point of Cause.

5. Origin: Finding the root cause of our problem.

6. Take Action: Prioritizing and executing an action plan to eliminate or reduce our gap through Long-Term countermeasures.

7. Monitor Effectiveness: Ensuring our actions had the intended effect of reducing the gap.

8. Standardize Success: Successful solutions are standardized and shared across the organization to prevent recurrence and to leverage learning.

Importance of Structure

A structured approach to problem-solving is crucial for several reasons:

1. Clarity and Focus: It helps teams to stay focused on the problem at hand and prevents them from getting sidetracked.

2. Efficiency: Streamlines the problem-solving process, making it more efficient and reducing the time to resolution. It also reduces work arounds and firefighting also known as short-term countermeasures.

3. Consistency: It ensures that problems across different teams or departments are approached in a consistent manner, facilitating learning and knowledge sharing.

4. Empowerment: A clear structure empowers team members by providing them with a proven framework to tackle problems, reducing reliance on management for solutions.

5. Continuous Improvement: Structured problem solving is iterative, enabling continuous refinements and leading to a culture of ongoing improvement.

6. Effective: Structured problem solving ensures that the actions taken are solving the root cause of the problem and then are monitored to ensure gap closure.

7. Reduces complexity: Large complex problems are systematically simplified until finding the root cause of the problem.

Support

To support practical problem solving, organizations must create structures that foster collaboration, learning, and rapid iteration. This involves:

1. Cross-Functional Teams: Bringing together diverse skill sets and perspectives to tackle problems more holistically.

2. Feedback Loops: Establishing mechanisms for regular feedback, allowing teams to adapt and iterate on their solutions quickly.

3. Supportive Infrastructure: Providing the necessary tools, time, and resources for teams to engage in problem-solving activities.

4. Learning Environment: Creating an organizational culture that values learning and development, encouraging teams to take calculated risks and learn from failures.

By emphasizing practical problem solving and structuring the organization to support it, businesses can cultivate a robust continuous improvement culture. This not only enhances problem-solving capabilities but also fosters a more engaged, empowered, and efficient workforce.

Company-Wide Rollout Strategies

The transition to a culture of continuous improvement is a strategic endeavor that requires thoughtful planning, committed leadership, and active participation from all members of the organization. All this being said, you can begin Problem Solving and using these Practical Problem-Solving techniques right now in any business whether it is a Lean business or not.

Leaders must not only endorse the continuous improvement initiative but also actively engage in its practices.

If you are tasked with a companywide continuous improvement or Lean rollout, these are some quick concepts to consider:

Leadership Commitment and Role Modeling

I am repeating this again, as it is so particularly important that at the forefront of this transformative journey is the unwavering commitment of the organization's leadership. Leaders must not only endorse the continuous improvement initiative but also actively engage in its practices. By participating in Lean activities and demonstrating a genuine dedication to the principles of continuous improvement, leaders serve as powerful role models, setting a precedent for the entire organization to follow.

Their visible commitment is crucial in signaling the importance of this cultural shift, thereby fostering an environment where continuous improvement is valued and pursued at all levels.

Tailored Communication and Engagement Plan

A successful rollout hinges on effective communication that resonates with the diverse audience within an organization. Developing a tailored communication and engagement plan ensures that the message of continuous improvement is not only heard but also embraced across the organization. This plan should articulate the benefits of adopting Lean principles, address potential concerns, and outline the positive changes that employees can expect. By making the communication relevant and engaging, the organization can secure buy-in from all stakeholders, paving the way for a smoother implementation process.

Training and Skill Development

To empower employees to contribute meaningfully to continuous improvement efforts, comprehensive training programs are essential. These programs should cover the fundamentals of Lean methodology and practical problem-solving techniques, providing employees with the tools they need to identify inefficiencies, devise innovative solutions, and implement changes effectively. Training should be tiered, offering basic Lean education for the wider workforce and more specialized training for those directly involved in continuous improvement projects. It must be understood that the best learning comes from doing. Many will not be 100% comfortable going into problem solving, however through doing problem solving they will gain the confidence and knowledge needed to solve the most troublesome and complex problems. Many companies train in problem solving prior to problem solving events, this helps new and more experienced employees to align on the process moving forward.

Pilot Projects

Beginning the rollout with carefully selected pilot projects allows the organization to evaluate and refine its approach to continuous improvement in a controlled environment. These pilot projects should aim for quick wins in areas where improvements can be readily achieved and measured. The success of these initial projects serves as a proof of concept, demonstrating the tangible benefits of continuous improvement and generating enthusiasm and support for broader implementation.

Infrastructure for Continuous Improvement

To sustain and support continuous improvement activities, it's vital to establish an infrastructure dedicated to overseeing these efforts. This could take the form of a Continuous Improvement Office or cross-functional teams tasked with facilitating improvement initiatives. This infrastructure acts as the backbone of the continuous improvement culture, providing the necessary resources, guidance, and oversight to ensure that improvement efforts are aligned with organizational goals and are executed efficiently.

Scaling and Integration

After demonstrating success with pilot projects, the next step is to scale and integrate continuous improvement practices throughout the organization. This phase involves customizing and adapting the approach to fit the unique needs and challenges of different departments and functions, ensuring that continuous improvement becomes an integral part of every aspect of the organization's operations.

Continuous Learning

To maintain the momentum of continuous improvement and ensure its long-term sustainability, it's crucial to establish feedback mechanisms or maturity tracking that allow for regular evaluation and adaptation of improvement activities. These feedback loops facilitate continuous learning, enabling the organization to respond dynamically to new challenges and opportunities for improvement.

Embracing Kaizen

At its core, Lean is about a relentless desire for improvement. It's a belief system that embraces the idea that the people closest to the work, who live through it every day, have the greatest insights on how to change and improve it. It's a philosophy that transforms every problem into an opportunity to grow and learn, and it is the engine that propels all steps to continuous improvement in the implementation of a lean culture.

Empowering the Workforce

This is another topic I will repeat and emphasize again and again and that is at the heart of effective problem-solving in a Lean environment is the active involvement of those who directly interact with the processes. Taking a bottom-up approach harnesses the collective wisdom and experience of the workforce and fosters ownership and engagement, rendering the journey of continuous improvement a shared one.

Conclusion

The journey towards a company-wide Lean transformation is undeniably complex and challenging. However, the key to success lies in starting small, with pilot projects that demonstrate quick wins and build momentum. These initial successes drew positive attention and excitement, guiding the scaling and integration of Lean practices across the organization, tailored to meet the unique needs and challenges of various departments and functions.

In essence, the transformation to a continuous improvement culture is a journey that never truly ends.

In essence, the transformation to a continuous improvement culture is a journey that never truly ends. It's an ongoing commitment to excellence, where every employee is empowered to contribute, every leader is a facilitator of change, and every challenge is an opportunity for growth. Let this journey begin with a single step, a small change, and a commitment to learning as you go, knowing that each step forward is a step towards a more efficient, empowered, and innovative organization.

CHAPTER 2
STORIES OF SUCCESS AND FAILURE

In the realm of Lean methodology, the path to continuous improvement is marked by both achievements and challenges. Each instance of success or failure serves as a vital learning opportunity, offering insights that propel further progress. This chapter compiles real-life experiences to capture the essence of Lean principles. Through these narratives, we delve into the transformative power of incremental changes, the significance of respecting and empowering individuals, and the profound impact of a culture dedicated to the relentless pursuit of perfection. These stories not only illustrate the practical application of Lean concepts but also reflect the enduring human spirit of innovation and resilience. I have gathered a brief collection of stories from my experiences over the years that have profoundly influenced my thinking and, in some instances, fundamentally altered the course of my life.

Origin Problem Solving | Dustin Thomas

TIME COMMITMENT

In the busy world of substation design, the relentless quest for efficiency often leads to one frustrating irony: remaining so entrenched in daily tasks that the time to deal with the very inefficiencies that consume us eludes us. In so many ways, this is the story of this paradox, where the commitment to solving problems gets overshadowed by the need to continue fighting each day to meet deadlines. A funny thing happened in this story and many other stories like it, an emerging shift in culture began to drive people to action. This story is about one person's passion for making things better that lit a clear path to resolution.

Roy J. Raines, a member of the Substation Design group, is a person who is never content with the way things are and it is that restlessness and yearning for change that despite a comfortable life in Mobile, Alabama, he felt a nagging sense of dissatisfaction with the status quo. Roy believed that true growth lay in embracing change and seeking out new challenges, a philosophy that often left him feeling out of sync with the more stable and contented mindset of his peers.

Roy felt trapped and helpless to remove waste that was occupying his time.

This relentless pursuit of personal and professional development eventually led him to make a significant life decision: relocating to Grand Rapids, Michigan. Roy saw in Grand Rapids an opportunity to not only advance his career in a fresh environment but also to immerse himself in a new community with different perspectives and challenges. After a few years he began to feel that very same unsettledness in his work in Grand Rapids that he had in Mobile. He was burdened with inefficient processes and saw significant waste, waste that if eliminated, could free countless hours of his team's time every month. Roy felt trapped and helpless to remove waste that was occupying his time. His previous interactions with leaders and coworkers were met with statements like "It is what it is" or "This is how we've always done it." But recently an emerging CEO had ushered in a shift in culture, driving a focus on enablement of its workforce. With this shift, new Lean leaders talked about enabling people who experience the problems the time to fix those same problems. Driven by a profound sense of responsibility and a "burning need to act" he took one of those problems he experienced to heart. However, he was acutely aware of the challenge ahead: finding a way to address the waste without disrupting the already packed schedules of his cross-functional team.

In search of a solution, Roy and I engaged in a strategic discussion, where we decided to leverage the power of a Kaizen event. This approach, known for its ability to foster quick, collaborative action, seemed perfectly suited to our needs. We planned to use practical problem solving as our guide

Sometimes, investing small amounts of time in problem-solving can lead to significant long-term gain.

utilizing a blank piece of A3 sized paper. This would allow us to visually chart our journey through the problem-solving steps. With a plan in hand, Roy took the reins and created a team. At first, the members were hesitant. The notion of another investment of time on top of their roles was daunting. Roy's leadership and the concentrated approach worked to alleviate those concerns. We ensured that we ran our meetings with efficiency and effectiveness. They were kept short and to a focused agenda that pushed our objective out the door. By breaking up the process into a few short meetings over the course of a week, we minimized the daily job impacts to the team.

The impact of this kind of a united front was nothing less than transformative. They had identified a process where they would create cells for a design and for every other design, create the same cells from beginning to end. Not only that, but different designers had diverse ways of approaching each cell. This process was tracked, and the data put it at a 2-hour average time of completion. Through practical problem solving we were able to standardize this process and move to a library, cutting this process time down to a *single minute*. This standardized process would save 32 hours per month.

By sharing a consistent approach to problem-solving and engaging in waste identification, we enabled the team to make small but meaningful changes. The use of the A3 document enabled the team to tell a compelling story of how they moved from the current state to the future state free from the shackles of overproduction, defects, and unnecessary movement. The team's adoption and commitment, along with the visual improvements to their process, offered a powerful reminder: Sometimes, investing small amounts of time in problem-solving can lead to significant long-term gain. Roy's leadership and the team's openness to change were proof that resolving problems is possible with the right mindset and a strategic approach. This story demonstrates the power each of us has to drive change that can do untold good, as long as we are willing to make the first leap to a better way.

Origin Problem Solving | Dustin Thomas

FOCUS ON THE PROCESS

In my history of problem-solving narratives, few are as compelling and enlightening as the story of the Trailer Fire Event—a saga that unfolds within the intricate weave of human resilience, collaborative spirit, and innovative thought. It was a lesson for me of how adversity, when approached with a mindset anchored in growth and unity, can unveil pathways to unforeseen solutions and forge a culture of trust and open communication.

One scorching summer day unfolded an event that, on the surface, bore the hallmarks of a distressing ordeal, an incident involving a trailer, its wheel bearing catastrophically failing, and the consequent inferno that ensued engulfing the trailer. The fire was finally put out and an unrecognizable black outline of what was once a semitrailer remained. There was first a sigh of relief that no one had been injured, but that relief would soon give way to a new kind of fear. At the heart of this turmoil was a Union coworker, ensnared in the chaos, her voice funneled through Union representation. The weight of blame loomed large, casting a cloud over two departments, each fearing the fallout. Yet, this narrative is set against the backdrop of a time when our Lean culture was in the process of taking root. This rising shift in culture

> *The weight of blame loomed large, casting a cloud over two departments, each fearing the fallout.*

morphs this from a tale of apprehension to one of transformative problem-solving.

Enter the scene, Daniel Tate and Zachary Cooper, our safety consultants, whose unwavering commitment to the well-being of our team has never been in question. I joined our safety consultants as the Lean consultant and together our presence was not just as overseers but as harbingers of a shift in perspective, a pivot from blaming to one that is process focused. Together, we recognized an invaluable opportunity: engage in practical problem solving, unearth the root cause, and forge a path to a robust solution, all while ensuring those most impacted by the event and the process led the charge.

The inaugural meeting was fragile but the initial steps of problem-solving were undertaken with a laser focus on the process. The air began to shift, once thick with defensiveness, gradually became imbued with a spirit of collaboration. Gone were the accusatory queries; in their place, inquiries that sought to understand the standard, its accessibility, and its adequacy. A sense of camaraderie was palpable, as Daniel, Zach, and I shared affirmations of our forward momentum.

Subsequent gatherings mirrored the success of the first, with our Union colleague now engaging openly, her insights proving invaluable. The Fleet's stance softened, transitioning from defensive to cooperative, while the Supply Chain team stood ready to lend their support. This collective endeavor was pivotal, not merely in bridging the immediate chasm but in fortifying our ranks against future adversities. This story in our journey exemplifies a crucial pivot, from a culture of blame to one of

Origin Problem Solving | Dustin Thomas

collective problem-solving. By centering on the process and delving into the root causes without casting aspersions on individuals, we cultivated an environment where change is not just welcomed but championed by all. While the details of the identified root causes and the subsequent action plans created to eliminate the issues are a distant memory, *and not the point of this or any of these stories*, what is still significantly memorable was that this event stood as a testament to the power of unity and trust in transforming challenges into opportunities for growth and improvement by creating a <u>culture</u> that is focused on the process and not on the individual.

Origin Problem Solving | Dustin Thomas

STANDARDS: A THIN LINE BETWEEN ORDER AND CHAOS

In the world of continuous improvement there is a mantra that I've shared throughout the corridors of industry: "We can't have a problem unless we have a standard." It is a principle that underpins the essence of continuous improvement. For without a baseline, improvement is but a mirage. However, the test of an assertion is not in what we say, rather what we do. And so, begins this short story where the absence of standards, or rather their inadequacy, beckoned a crisis of great proportions.

The incident occurred among the dust and dinge of a shop floor in the stages of renovation and transformation. It was here a blade met the unsuspecting resistance of an underground electrical cable. This was no mere mishap but a larger potential catastrophe. The severing of the cable was a brush with disaster, for the thought of injury, or worse, loomed large. Tension made the atmosphere thick and accusations ripe. A construction worker, following instructions, unwittingly was put in grave danger. The project manager reciprocated, redirecting his scorn to a ground penetrating radar technician who had scanned the location days prior. This is the point where I entered the mix. The culture of blame is a demon to which I had, over the years, been unceremoniously introduced. It is a villain,

It was here a blade met the unsuspecting resistance of an underground electrical cable.

but I knew its tricks and had the key to its lair. In years past, this situation would have resulted in disciplinary actions for all involved and maliciously would not have resulted in any real actions to prevent it from happening again. But now, after our culture shifted to that of standard creation and revision, the tools for understanding the process and its standards resided in my arsenal.

Our journey took us from the sterile confines of the conference room to the heart of the shop floor as part of a *Go and See* (Go to the Gemba) or otherwise said simply, to go to the shop floor and observe. It was here, amidst the concrete and steel, with standards in tow, that the story began to reveal its hand. A request form for ground-penetrating radar, once deemed detailed, now revealed its ambiguity. It was a map that led nowhere, a guide that spoke in generalities. This revelation was one puzzle piece among many pieces that laid scattered. Because we went to the shop floor and because we had standards with us, we were able to see those pieces start to come together. Among them were last-minute changes, previously unpredictable situations, and visual deficiencies. Armed with new insight, we set out to rewrite the rules of engagement and ensure that this problem would never happen again by revising our standards and refining our processes.

This quick story of the constant struggle between chaos and order serves as a reminder. A reminder that the foundation of improvement is not just in the standards we set but in our unyielding commitment to scrutinize, adapt, and continuously improve them.

Origin Problem Solving | Dustin Thomas

GO AND SEE

I spoke briefly in the last story of Go and See and in this story, I will explain how one Go and See helped change my eventual entire career path.

Skepticism and frustration were our initial companions, for what more could we glean from a sight so familiar, a battle so frequently fought?

In the heart of an industrial colossus, amidst the relentless hum of machinery, my journey as a young production supervisor began. Entrusted with the stewardship of two gargantuan recycled paperboard machines, I was the architect of the very footing of everyday life: cereal boxes, pizza boxes, the unsung heroes of the breakfast table and late-night cravings. Fresh from the vigor of a Lean initiative rollout, skepticism clouded my enthusiasm. To me, it was yet another fleeting corporate crusade. Yet, little did I know, I was on the cusp of a revelation that would not only solve a pressing enigma but also ignite a lifelong passion for Lean principles. Our adversary was elusive, a defect that manifested as wrinkles in the paper, wreaking havoc and incurring losses that ran into tens of thousands of dollars, sometimes daily. Despite our best efforts, the solution remained just beyond our grasp, a puzzle wrapped in the roar of the machines. We lived through this problem, breathed it, and yet, it continued to elude us.

The concept of "Go and See" was whispered among us, a mantra from the Lean lexicon that beckoned us to venture beyond the confines of theory and into the very heart of our operations. Skepticism and frustration were our initial companions, for what more could we glean from a sight so familiar, a battle so frequently fought? We paused our discussions confined to our conference room and then dressed in the armor of our trade, hard hats, earplugs, and safety glasses. We then stepped from the sanctuary of our air-conditioned Problem-Solving event and into the sweltering reality of the production floor. It was a realm of heat and noise, where machines loomed like industrial titans, their roars a constant challenge to our resolve. Yet, in this incursion, my purpose was transformed. No longer was I there to command or to cure, I was an observer, a seeker of truth. As coached, I would ask questions only to understand and observe operators only to gain perspective.

The paper machine, a leviathan of steel, stretched before us, its heart beating with the rhythm of production. The coater machine, with its dual applicators and cavernous oven, stood as a testament to human ingenuity. Yet, it was in the intricate details that our salvation lay hidden. An adjustment wheel, unnoticed in the years of rou-

No longer was I there to command or to cure, I was an observer, a seeker of truth.

tine, caught my eye, a beacon in the darkness. Caked with decades worth of coating it was almost impossible to see, camouflaged into its surroundings. The operator initiated the sequence to bring all the rolls and pans into position. With patience we watched, and there it was—a slight unevenness, a precursor to the chaos that ensued. The bead of coating, an anomaly in the dance of machinery, was the harbinger of our downfall. Ever so slightly the far end of the applicator roll had touchdown first, it wasn't obvious, but it was enough. In that moment of clarity, time stood still. The wrinkles, our relentless foe, unfolded before us, not as a specter to be feared, but as a secret that was unraveling. The problem that had haunted our days and nights untangled; its solution not yet completely understood but confidence flowed from us. It was a victory not just over a technical challenge, but over the malaise of our own skepticism.

The "Go and See" philosophy transcended its initial guise as a mere Lean tool, becoming a source of enlightenment. That day marked the beginning of a transformation, not just in our processes, but in my very approach to problem-solving and leadership. The fire that was lit within me propelled me on a journey of discovery. I emerged not just as a supervisor, but as a disciple of a philosophy that champions observation, humility, and the relentless pursuit of excellence. The wrinkles on the paperboard were ironed out, but the lessons learned would change the direction of my entire career.

DEATH OF A FRIEND

In the dimly lit corridors of a sprawling industrial complex, where the incessant hum of machinery filled the air, I as a young engineer navigating the labyrinth of steel and steam. Driven by ambition and the unspoken codes of the industry, I witnessed the dance of near misses and shrugged-off warnings that were part of the daily grind.

One fateful day, the delicate balance of hazard and neglect was shattered. It began with a scream. A fellow supervisor, Jamie, a friend and at times even a mentor, fell victim to an ill-conceived standard that had promised efficiency but delivered peril. Trapped by the very machine he sought to master, Jamie's ordeal was not an immediate surrender but a dreadful, prolonged, and ugly battle, a horrific tableau that unfolded before my eyes.

> *One fateful day, the delicate balance of hazard and neglect was shattered.*

Haunted by the traumatic demise of Jamie, my dreams became a theater for replaying the nightmare, the screams, the images, the panic, the fear, all a stark, unyielding reminder of the day the industrial beast claimed a life. What emerged was a crucible for me, searing away picturesque naivety in favor of a resolve coarsely honed with the lessons of reality.

With time, I rose through the ranks, but the ascent was shadowed by the weight of that tragic memory. It became clear that the prevailing approach to problem-solving in this industrial behemoth was a reactive one, a cycle of Band-Aid solutions applied only after wounds were inflicted. But the cost of such lessons was steep, paid in the currency of human lives and suffering.

Determined to chart a new course, I and others with me, became an advocate for a culture of foresight, where potential dangers were not merely noted but actively neutralized before they could wreak havoc. Emphasizing the importance of risk assessment, we led initiatives to dissect processes and identify the lurking threats, advocating for strategies to preemptively disarm them.

Embracing the principles of continuous improvement, we championed Lean and Six Sigma, weaving them into the fabric of the organization. These were not just methodologies but a new creed, a way to imbue the organization with an ethos of relentless optimization and safety.

Understanding that true change needed allies, we focused on empowering the workforce. Training programs were overhauled to do more than just instruct; they aimed to empower every worker with the knowledge and authority to challenge unsafe practices and halt operations if danger loomed. Safety was no longer the sole domain of supervisors; it became everyone's duty to bear.

Technological advancements became tools in our crusade. Sensors and analytics, once mere facets of productivity, were repurposed to serve as the complex's nervous system, alerting to the slightest hint of malfunction or threat.

Origin Problem Solving | Dustin Thomas

In this narrative of transformation, we attempted to honor Jamie's memory not through words of mourning but through actions that spoke of learning and prevention. It was a testament to the belief that the path to innovation and progress should never be paved with the well-being of the workforce. In the end, this story is a call for vigilance and a commitment to a future where industrial nightmares are relics of the past, and safety is the cornerstone of all endeavors.

In industrial settings and in much of life and business, nearly all problem solving is reactive: an event occurs, and we take measures to prevent that specific event from recurring. But this strategy is limited by design. It requires that we learn from failure, and my experience of loss underscores how painful some of that learning can be. Proactive problem solving, however, involves efforts to anticipate and mitigate problems before they occur. It requires a continuous effort of looking forward, assessing risk, and implementing strategies to prevent those risks from manifesting as real problems. It involves a culture that doesn't wait for problems to occur; it actively seeks to prioritize and mitigate the risks that could lead to those problems.

in the quest to improve and innovate, the highest priority must always be the safety and well-being of the people involved.

This seems as good a time as any to discuss how organizations can invest in culture, systems, training, which anticipate rather than react. These might include:

- Risk Assessment and Management: Regularly analyzing processes to identify potential risks and implementing strategies to mitigate them before they lead to incidents.

- Continuous Improvement: Adopting frameworks like Lean or Six Sigma that embed the principles of ongoing improvement and proactive problem-solving into the fabric of an organization.

- Employee Training and Engagement: Empowering workers at all levels with the knowledge and authority to identify, address potential risks, and ultimately stop or suspend any job at any moment, ensuring that safety and proactive problem-solving are everyone's responsibility.

- Technological Solutions: Leveraging technology to monitor processes and predict potential failures before they occur, from sophisticated analytics to AI sensors.

In remembering my friend and the circumstances that led to his loss, I want to highlight a critical lesson for all of us: the importance of vigilance, foresight, and a commitment to safety. I plead for a powerful call to action for organizations to prioritize the safety and well-being of their employees above all else. It's a poignant reminder that in the quest to improve and innovate, the highest priority must always be the safety and well-being of the people involved.

Problems don't always immediately rear their ugly head, many times we experience their first soft touches and it's in those instances we need to take notice.

CHAPTER 3
THE 8 STEPS OVERVIEW

When it comes to Lean problem-solving, we're not just talking about a quick fix, firefighting, or short-term countermeasures. It's about eliminating the problem at the root. It is a thorough exploration that demands a methodical approach to navigate each step of the problem-solving framework with precision. Let's embark on this journey.

Preparation: Laying the Groundwork for Success

First things first, preparation is key. It's like setting the stage before the big show. Here, we pinpoint the problem owner, the person with the reins, ready to lead the charge. Gathering a diverse team comes next, ensuring we've got a mix of expertise and perspectives to tackle the issue from all angles. And data? We're hoarding it, every bit of info and historical data that shines a light on what we're up against.

Perception: Understanding the Problem

Now, it's time to get a clear yet general understanding of the beast we're facing. It's about painting a picture of the problem, touching on the who, what, where, and when. Crafting a precise problem statement is crucial here, along with understanding why this challenge is worth our sweat.

Define our Problem

Here, we're setting the battlefield. What's the target, and where do we stand now? This step is about measuring the mountain we've got to climb, setting clear success metrics, and understanding the gap between where we are and where we need to be.

Breaking Down the Problem

Think of this as dissecting the problem into bite-sized pieces. We're using data to chop it up into manageable chunks and then picking our battles, focusing on the segments that pack the biggest punch or have the easiest wins.

Identify and Locate: SMART Target and POC

After breaking the problem down into chunks, we then choose a problem and set a SMART target. We also identify the location this problem is originating from within the process.

Origin: Root Cause Analysis

This is where the detective work comes in. We're digging deep, peeling back the layers to uncover what's really fueling this fire. Tools like the 5 Whys or the Fishbone Diagram are our best friends here, guiding us to the root cause(s).

Take Action: Crafting and Implementing Solutions

Armed with insights and a clear target, it's time to get our hands dirty. We're brainstorming solutions, drawing from the best practices and a sprinkle of innovation. Then, it's all about meticulous planning, laying out the steps, resources, and timelines to bring our chosen solutions to life.

Monitoring Effectiveness: Evaluating Impact

With the solutions in play, we're keeping a close eye on their performance. Are we hitting the mark? Using the metrics we defined earlier, we're tracking progress and ensuring we're closing the gap effectively.

Standardizing Success

Last but definitely not least, we're locking in our wins. By standardizing the successful strategies and setting up a framework for continuous monitoring and improvement, we're making sure today's solutions stand the test of time, keeping the problem at bay for good.

Embarking on this journey demands more than just a set of steps; it requires a mindset geared towards meticulous analysis, creative solutioning, and continuous improvement. Each phase is a building block, setting the foundation for a robust, Lean problem-solving approach that's as much about the destination as it is about the journey.

The Multifaceted Landscape of Problem Solving

The realm of problem solving is as diverse as it is dynamic, with a myriad of methodologies and frameworks developed across various sectors, companies, and even over time. This diversity often leads to an array of problem-solving approaches, each with its unique set of steps, terminologies, and focal points. As one embarks on the journey of mastering problem-solving skills, it becomes evident that the specific labeling and sequence of steps can vary significantly from one approach to another.

Despite the superficial differences in the problem-solving approaches encountered across different contexts, the underlying journey remains consistent. This universal journey through problem solving underscores the fundamental process of identifying, analyzing, and addressing issues, regardless of the specific labels or steps involved. The essence of problem-solving lies not in the individual steps but in the holistic journey of moving from problem identification to solution implementation and beyond.

Drawing from roughly two decades of experience in the field of problem solving, this book presents a carefully curated 8-step approach that has been honed to effectively tackle problems. This approach, while unique in its composition, is rooted in the universal principles of problem solving, offering a robust framework that balances practicality with depth.

One such notable deviation from many conventional problem-solving frameworks is the treatment of short-term countermeasures. While commonly featured as a distinct step in many methodologies, this approach reevaluates their role and utility in the problem-solving process. Short-term countermeasures, though potentially useful in certain contexts, are often seen as merely a documentation of current practices or, in some cases, a diversion from the long-term objectives of problem solving. The perspective offered here suggests that short-term countermeasures, while part of the problem-solving journey, are best integrated into the preparation phase rather than highlighted as a focal point during the event. This approach stems from the belief that the emphasis on short-term solutions can sometimes overshadow the pursuit of more sustainable, long-term improvements.

Embracing Flexibility and Continuous Improvement

For those who may already be accustomed to a different 8-step standard, this book does not advocate for a complete overhaul of established methodologies. Instead, it encourages readers to integrate the insights and strategies presented here into their existing frameworks, enhancing and continuously improving upon their current problem-solving practices. The goal is not to replace but to enrich and expand the repertoire of problem-solving tools at one's disposal.

In the ever-evolving landscape of problem solving, the diversity of approaches reflects the complexity and variability of the challenges faced. The 8-step approach outlined in this book is offered not as the definitive method but as a refined pathway forged through years of practice, inviting readers to adapt, integrate, and evolve their problem-solving strategies in the pursuit of excellence.

Just Do It

Before we move forward, it is crucial to differentiate between immediate corrective actions, often referred to as "Just Do It" (JDI), and practical problem-solving methods. The PDCA (Plan-Do-Check-Act) cycle remains integral to both approaches.

"**Just Do It**" is immediate corrective action taken when a problem arises that meets specific criteria:

- The problem is not repetitive, where you have attempted to fix before and it returned.
- The problem is simple.
- The root cause is obvious.
- There is unanimous agreement on the solution.

When these conditions are met, the problem should be addressed immediately without extensive analysis. This approach ensures that small, simple issues are resolved quickly, maintaining operational efficiency.

While JDI actions are prompt and straightforward, they still fit within the PDCA framework. Here's how:

1. **Plan**:
    - **Identification**: Recognize the issue that requires a JDI approach. This includes understanding the problem's context and confirming it meets the JDI criteria.
    - **Agreement**: Ensure there is a consensus on the problem and its obvious solution.
2. **Do**:
    - **Implementation**: Execute the immediate corrective action to address the problem. This stage focuses on swift resolution without detailed analysis or

planning, leveraging the simplicity and obviousness of the solution.

3. **Check**:

    o **Verification**: Even though the problem is resolved, it's essential to verify the effectiveness of the action taken. This ensures that the immediate fix has indeed addressed the issue without unintended consequences.

    o **Documentation**: Record the problem and the action taken for future reference and to aid in recognizing patterns if similar issues arise.

4. **Act**:

    o **Standardization**: If the action was effective and the problem is unlikely to recur, standardize the solution. This involves incorporating the immediate fix into routine procedures to prevent similar issues in the future.

    o **Review**: If the problem reoccurs, it signals a need to move beyond JDI and employ a more detailed problem-solving approach, possibly revisiting the PDCA cycle with a more in-depth analysis.

Not all problems can be resolved through immediate corrective actions. If a problem does not meet the JDI criteria, it is essential to engage in practical problem-solving from the start.

CHAPTER 4
STEP 0: PREPARATION

The journey of problem-solving, many times, involves planning for the problem-solving event. The complexity of the problem and the deadline for impactful improvements will likely dictate how much or how little we need to prepare for the event itself. If this is a simpler problem or a problem that has no established deadline for resolution, then simply assigning team members and an owner is all that may be necessary to begin the journey. You would discover the data as needed and pull in additional team members when required as well as schedule sessions upon availability. At the other end of this spectrum would be tight deadlines, complex problems, and higher tensions. This type of event would call for establishing a backbone of the journey by completing steps before hand to understand what data is necessary to bring to the event as well as being rigorous in ownership and establishing a specific approach. The first step, often dictating the trajectory and success of the endeavor, is laying a solid groundwork. This chapter explores the quintessential phase of preparation, a step frequently overlooked, yet pivotal in setting the stage for effective problem resolution. In the realm of problem-solving, where challenges are multifaceted and solutions are not one-size-fits-all, the preparation phase becomes the bedrock upon which successful strategies are built. I will cover a lot of topics in this preparation section, and it will be up to YOU to decide what is needed for each problem-solving event.

Preparation transcends mere logistical readiness, embodying strategic alignment of resources, people, and data. This alignment ensures a cohesive approach to the problem at hand, optimizing the problem-solving process from the outset. Within this foundational phase, several key activities are

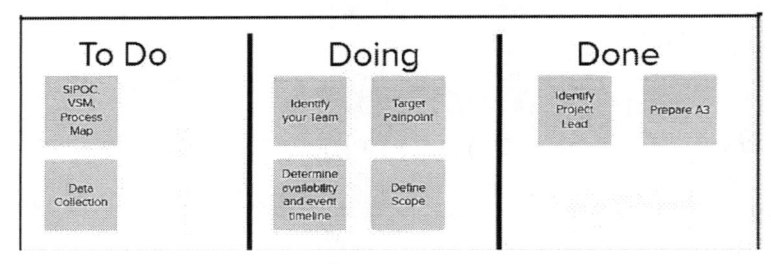

To Do	Doing	Done
SIPOC, VSM, Process Map	Identify your Team / Target Painpoint	Identify Project Lead / Prepare A3
Data Collection	Determine availability and event timeline / Define Scope	

designed, each with the objective of laying a solid foundation for the forthcoming stages of problem resolution. The initial task in this preparatory phase is establishing a clear structure to track progress. Employing a simple yet effective system of categorization such as 'To Do', 'Doing', and 'Done', provides a powerful tool for monitoring the evolution of tasks from inception to completion. Tailoring this structural framework to fit the specific nuances of the problem-solving event is essential, ensuring both flexibility and relevance.

A cornerstone of preparation is the identification and establishment of clear leadership. This role, typically assumed by a project lead or facilitator, is pivotal in navigating the complexities of the problem and maintaining team momentum. The early establishment of leadership imbues the team with direction and clarity, setting a tone of purpose and focus. Subsequent to defining leadership, the assembly of a diverse and competent team becomes the next order of business. This team, ideally comprising individuals directly impacted by the problem, brings to the table a wealth of practical experience and firsthand insights. For a more methodical approach, it is recommended that a SIPOC be completed in order to understand the people who are impacted through determining the Suppliers and Customers around the process. In the next Chapter I will detail more on how a SIPOC is completed and other ways it can be used.

Here are the key roles typically involved:

1. **Owner**: The central figure responsible for organizing and managing the event. The Owner ensures that all preparations are made before the event and oversees the execution of the problem-solving process.

2. **Facilitator**: This role, sometimes fulfilled by the Owner, is crucial for guiding the team through the structured problem-solving steps. The Facilitator helps maintain focus, pulls the team back on track if discussions deviate, and provides answers to procedural questions.

3. **Champion**: A key figure who, whether directly involved in the problem-solving event or not, is kept up to date through Charter signing and report outs. The Champion has the necessary authority to enforce countermeas-

ures and resolve escalated issues, particularly in cross-functional situations.

4. **Sponsor**: Usually a manager or executive, the Sponsor authorizes the time and resources dedicated to solving the problem. They formalize the commitment through the Charter and participate in the final report out, ensuring alignment with organizational goals.

5. **Team Members**: Comprising individuals or experts who directly interact with the problem. They bring firsthand experience and knowledge to the table, contributing to both the identification of the issue and the development of effective solutions.

0. PREPARATION

Owner:	Dustin Thomas
Champion:	Gordie Howe
Sponsor:	Wayne G. (Plant Manager)
Team:	Bobby Orr (machine 1 op), Bobby Hull (Asst), Mark Messier (hand), Steve Y (hand)

The mandatory positions necessary for problem solving are the Owner and the Team where additional positions are scaled with the complexity and risk involved in the problem being solved. Here is a chart depicting general time spent engaged in the problem-solving effort.

Position	Percent Time Engaged
Owner	100%
Facilitator	90-100%
Champion	20-90%
Sponsor	10%
Team	80-90%

Circle of Influence

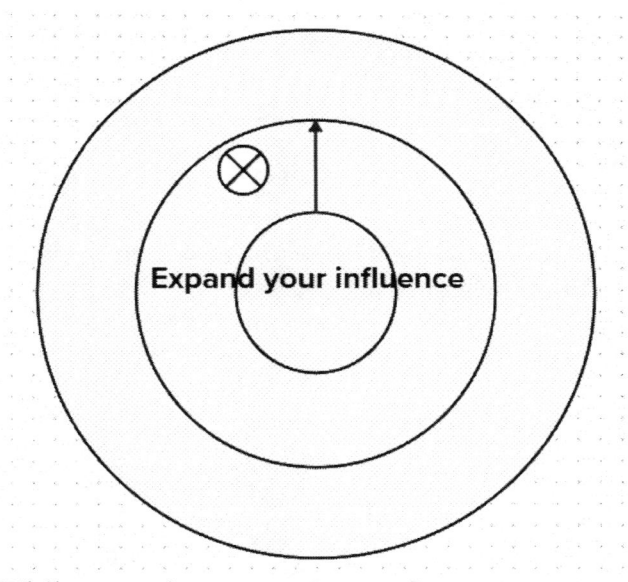

Expand your influence

While creating your team, I want to touch on a question I frequently encounter. I am often confronted with questions surrounding problems that lie outside of a department that struggles with defects downstream or people who want to solve problems outside their expertise or influence. They wonder how they can solve such problems. My answer is always that you cannot solve problems without the people engaged in the processes where the problem originates. When thinking about this, I often refer to Stephen Covey's Circle of Influence.

If your problem is outside of your Circle of Influence, then you *cannot solve it* unless you expand your influence. To do this, you will need to reach out to those necessary in order to expand your circle of influence. This could involve engaging with an additional department or enlisting specific Champions to assist in the solution rollout. This does not mean solving problems for other people, but it does mean that cross-functional leadership is often essential for moving forward efficiently and effectively.

Charter

A Charter is a formal agreement between the Owner and the Sponsor of what the Problem-Solving event will accomplish as well as a reference during the event. This is typically a dollar amount of savings, either hard savings or soft savings. It can be Unit Cost or general process efficiencies. Typically, process efficiencies are calculated based on soft savings from the reduction of struggle or hours saved through improvements. It could also be targets such as recordable injuries or quality improvements. The Charter will also outline the purpose, scope, objectives and participants of the event. Although everything here isn't needed in a charter, here are a few key components with explanations:

Purpose: At the heart of any event lies its purpose, which should spotlight the specific issue or challenge at hand. This isn't just about naming the event but diving into the 'why', what's the driving force behind gathering everyone together?

Scope: It's like drawing an invisible line around our problem-solving playground. This defines what's in play and what's out, helping us keep our eyes on the ball without getting sidetracked by issues that aren't our focus for the day.

Objectives: Here's where we get down to brass tacks. Setting goals isn't just about wishful thinking; it's about laying down concrete, achievable targets that align with our purpose. These goals are our north star, guiding every discussion and decision.

Participants: This is our roll call – who's in the room? From the thinkers and the doers to the decision-makers, understanding the role and responsibility of each participant clarifies how everyone contributes to the event's success. If you're looking for an ideal team size, then I usually offer this: 4 – 8 team members, not including the facilitator. This does not mean 3 or 10 members is wrong, but I want to ensure you are not working on processes that aren't represented by team members and balancing that with not including too many team members that often result in too many opinions and too much time spent agreeing on efforts.

Agenda: Think of this as our event blueprint, mapping out every discussion, break, and brainstorming session. It's about structuring our time together so that every crucial topic gets its moment in the spotlight.

Resources: Just like any quest needs its tools and maps, our event needs resources. Pinpointing what we have and what we need, be it information, tools, or expertise ensures we're well-equipped to tackle our challenges head-on.

Ground Rules: Setting the stage for how we interact, ground rules foster a space where ideas can flow freely, and respect is the name of the game. It's about creating a culture of constructive dialogue and mutual respect.

Methodology: This is our game plan—the strategies and techniques we'll employ to dissect problems, spark creativity, and find solutions. Whether it's a structured analysis or free-flowing ideation, choosing the right approach is key to our problem-solving journey.

Expected Outcomes: What's our finish line? It's about defining what success looks like, whether in the form of actionable plans, concrete decisions, or innovative solutions. These outcomes are our event's legacy, shaping what comes next.

Follow-up: The end of the event isn't the end of the road. Outlining next steps for implementation and accountability ensures that today's ideas become tomorrow's actions, keeping the momentum going and the progress on track.

Kaizen

Integral to the preparatory phase is the readiness of tools and frameworks that will be employed throughout the problem-solving journey. Whether digital platforms for collaboration or physical tools like whiteboards and A3 documents, ensuring these tools are at hand is pivotal for a seamless flow of activities. Developing or gathering process maps such value stream maps, flowcharts, or SIPOC diagrams plays a significant role in this phase. These visual representations not only help define the scope of the problem but also ensure a unified understanding among team members. Before diving into the main problem-solving event, an initial analysis is sometimes conducted. This analysis involves a meticulous collection of relevant data, setting the stage for informed decision-making and ensuring the team is well-equipped to tackle the problem with insight. With the foundational elements in place, attention shifts to the scheduling of the problem-solving event. This entails aligning team member availability with a realistic and comprehensive timeline, paving the way for an in-depth exploration and resolution of the problem. There should be some thought about how to approach the timeline.

My personal opinion is a condensed timeline, also known as a Kaizen approach. Kaizen, a Japanese term for "change for the better," reflects a philosophy of continuous, incremental improvement and is a cornerstone in the landscape of operational excellence. The Kaizen event, a focused, short-term project to improve a specific process or issue, embodies this philosophy through a structured, week-long endeavor aimed at problem-solving and process improvement. This chapter delineates a typical five-day Kaizen event, breaking down the activities and objectives for each day to provide a clear roadmap for execution. Preparation for this

SUNDAY	MONDAY	TUESDAY	WEDNESDAY	THURSDAY	FRIDAY	SATURDAY
	7AM - 9AM	7AM - 9AM	7AM - 8AM	7AM - 8AM	7AM - 8AM	
	2PM - 4PM	2PM - 4PM	8AM - 10A	8AM - 4PM	8AM - 10A	
			2PM - 4PM		1PM - 2PM	

event would typically take 1-2 weeks or less depending on how much data is readily available. Preparation is key for a Kaizen event. A typical schedule after preparation would look like the following:

Day 1: Setting the Stage

The first day of the Kaizen event is pivotal, setting the tone for the week ahead. The morning is dedicated to introducing the problem at hand and providing training on the practical problem-solving standard. This dual focus ensures that all participants start with a common understanding of the problem and the methodologies to be employed, leveling the knowledge base and refreshing memories.

Afternoon: Diving into Problem Identification

Post-training, the afternoon session transitions into the active problem-solving phase, covering Steps 1 through 3 of the methodology. The aim is to end the day with a well-defined, specific problem that the team will address over the course of the event. This phase involves identifying, clarifying, and scoping the problem, ensuring that the team has a clear target for their improvement efforts.

SUNDAY	MONDAY	TUESDAY	WEDNESDAY	THURSDAY	FRIDAY	SATURDAY
	Introduction and Training	Step 4 & 5 Find the root cause		Step 7 Monitor Success	Report out on Current Results of activities	
			Step 6 Execute Action plan		Prepare and practice Executive presentation	
	Steps 1-3 Selecting the problem(s) to solve	Step 6 Develop Action Plan		Execute on any findings from Step 7		
					Report out to Sponsor	

Day 2: Analysis and Planning

With a specific problem in hand, Day 2 starts with establishing a SMART Target—Specific, Measurable, Achievable, Relevant, and Time-bound—for the issue. The morning's efforts are centered on drilling down to the root cause of the problem, utilizing tools and techniques that facilitate deep analysis.

Afternoon: Solution Development

The latter half of the day is dedicated to ideating solutions, prioritizing them based on impact and feasibility, and then developing a comprehensive action plan. This stage is critical as it translates insights and analysis into actionable steps that the team will undertake to address the identified problem.

Day 3: Execution

The third day is all about action—implementing the plans crafted on Day 2. This day emphasizes effective and efficient execution, with the team working collaboratively to bring their proposed solutions to life. The focus is on tangible progress and overcoming any immediate challenges that arise during implementation.

Day 4: Monitoring and Adjustment

Following the execution phase, Day 4 revolves around monitoring the effectiveness of the implemented solutions and making necessary adjustments. The team assesses the impact of their actions, comparing against the SMART Target set earlier and determining any additional measures required to achieve the desired outcomes.

Day 5: Review and Reporting

The final day is a time for reflection, analysis, and communication. The team reviews all data collected from the execution and monitoring phases, making any last-minute adjustments to their plans. The culmination of the week's efforts is the Sponsor report-out—a comprehensive presentation detailing the journey undertaken, showcasing the latest data, and setting expectations for the outcomes and progress of the implemented plan.

The Kaizen event officially concludes with the Team report-out session, where the team addresses any questions from the Sponsor. This session also serves as an opportunity for the facilitator to formally transition the ongoing responsibility of the project to the Owner and Champion. This handover ensures that the improvements made during the event are sustained and that any additional action plans necessary to meet the targets are carried out.

In conclusion, a Kaizen event encapsulates the spirit of continuous improvement through a structured, intensive week of problem-solving and process enhancement. By adhering to a clear, day-by-day plan, teams can tackle specific issues with a concerted effort, leading to meaningful improvements.

Short-term Countermeasures

In the pursuit of operational excellence, the allure of short-term countermeasures often presents a deceptive solution to pressing problems. These immediate actions, typically celebrated as quick fixes or heroic firefighting, might temporarily 'stop the bleed' but often fall short of addressing the underlying issues. The narrative of top-down management applying band-aid solutions exemplifies this approach, where the immediate relief from an operational hiccup leads to convoluted processes and workarounds that linger far beyond their utility.

The reliance on short-term countermeasures, while initially gratifying, tends to embed inefficiencies within the system. Workarounds put in place by well-intentioned leaders or operators frequently become ingrained in daily operations, obscuring the root cause and complicating the process landscape. Over time, the origins of these makeshift solutions fade, leaving behind a legacy of complexity with no one to recount their inception or purpose.

The reliance on short-term countermeasures, while initially gratifying, tends to embed inefficiencies within the system.

Reflecting on early career experiences, the act of firefighting—swiftly addressing issues with temporary fixes—once seemed synonymous with effective problem-solving. However, the recurring nature of these problems reveals a fundamental flaw in this approach. True problem-solving extends beyond the immediate cessation of symptoms, aiming instead for a sustainable resolution that prevents recurrence.

The Proper Place

Short-term countermeasures are not without merit; they serve critical roles in preventing immediate financial loss, safeguarding against environmental disasters, or complying with legal obligations. Their implementation is often necessary to avert immediate harm or disruption. However, their application should be judicious, reserved for situations where immediate action is indispensable. With this in mind, these actions are then done in the preparation phase of problem solving or even before that at the time of problem occurrence.

In the formal journey of problem-solving, dedicating time to document and debate on short-term countermeasures can be counterproductive. If such measures were essential, they would likely have been implemented by the time problem-solving efforts are underway. The focus, instead, should be on uncovering and addressing the root cause, ensuring the deployment of long-term solutions that eradicate the problem at its source.

> *temporary solutions might bridge the gap until permanent fixes are realized.*

The notion of making short-term countermeasures deliberately painful, as I have heard many times, to prevent their permanence is fraught with paradox. This approach, while intended to deter reliance on temporary fixes, inadvertently adds complexity and discomfort without contributing to a lasting resolution. Thus, the true path to problem-solving may lie in resisting the temptation to employ short-term fixes unless absolutely necessary.

There are also instances where short-term countermeasures play a strategic role, particularly during the 'Take Action' phase of problem-solving. Once the root cause *has been identified* and a plan of action established, temporary solutions might bridge the gap until permanent fixes are realized. This approach ensures continuity and stability while the foundational issues are being systematically addressed.

Short-term countermeasures, while occasionally necessary, should not overshadow the core objective of problem-solving: to identify and resolve the root cause of issues for long-term improvement. By shifting the focus from firefighting to foundational solutions, we pave the way for sustainable operational excellence.

A3: The Problem-Solving Canvas

The A3 embodies a profound approach to problem solving. Named after the international paper size it traditionally occupies (roughly 11.5" x 16.5"), the A3 transcends its physical dimensions to represent a dynamic framework for navigating complex problems.

The real value of the A3 lies in the problem-solving process it facilitates, not in the physical layout

At its core, an A3 is a blank canvas, a starting point for documenting the journey through the structured process of problem solving. This simplicity is its strength, offering a versatile space that can adapt to the specific needs of each problem-solving endeavor, whether it's laid out on an actual piece of paper, a whiteboard, or a digital platform.

In the quest for standardization, many organizations adopt rigidly structured templates for problem solving, often packed with predefined fields and prompts. While these templates aim to guide users through the process, they inadvertently constrain thinking and creativity. The act of filling in predefined boxes can stifle the nuanced understanding and deep analysis required for effective problem solving, reducing it to a mechanical exercise devoid of genuine insight. The real value of the A3 lies in the problem-solving process it facilitates, not in the physical layout or structure of the document. The standardization that truly matters is the adherence to a disciplined, thoughtful approach to identifying, analyzing, and resolving problems, which the practical problem-solving process embodies. This process encourages a holistic view, prompting users to delve deeply into

Resorting to overly templated solutions prematurely can hinder the development of a mature problem-solving culture within an organization.

the context, causes, and potential solutions of the issue at hand.

While there may be cases where low-complexity issues with straightforward causes can be efficiently captured within a more structured template that utilizes practical problem solving, such simplicity should be approached with caution. Resorting to overly templated solutions prematurely can hinder the development of a mature problem-solving culture within an organization. The indiscriminate use of fill-in-the-blank templates can impede the growth of problem-solving skills among employees. Without the necessity to engage deeply with each step of the process, the understanding of the 'why' behind actions remains superficial, leading to mediocre solutions and a weakening of problem-solving culture. The A3, with its open format, encourages a more thoughtful, engaged approach, fostering a deeper understanding and more effective problem solving.

The A3, in its unassuming simplicity, is a powerful tool for fostering a culture of effective problem solving. It serves not just as a template but as a canvas for critical thinking, encouraging users to engage fully with the problem-solving process. By prioritizing the process over rigid structures, organizations can cultivate a workforce adept at navigating complex challenges, ensuring that problem-solving efforts yield meaningful, sustainable solutions. Leverage an A3 to document your progress and utilize your A3 as a means to communicate your journey. It serves both as your guide and as your narrative to convey and share.

CHAPTER 5
STEP 1: PERCEPTION

Perception is the lens through which we view and understand the problem. It encompasses the who, what, where, when, and crucially, why the issue at hand is significant. This step is not about delving into the root causes but rather framing the problem in a way that aligns all participants and provides a clear, concise overview for anyone reviewing the documentation of the problem-solving process. A well-articulated perception statement serves as the rallying point, drawing everyone's focus to the common challenge. It ensures that the team's efforts are synchronized and that the problem is presented in a manner easily understood by all stakeholders.

It is not uncommon for team members to enter a problem-solving event with differing views on the issue at hand. This diversity of perspective, while valuable, can initially pose a challenge in aligning the team's focus. The task of synthesizing these varying viewpoints into a cohesive problem statement is crucial. To navigate the complexities of team alignment, a structured approach to defining the problem proves invaluable. This involves methodically addressing the foundational questions of Who, What, Where, When and Why *is this important*. These questions serve as the pillars upon which a shared understanding can be constructed, providing a framework for the team to collectively explore and agree upon the problem's dimensions.

Who: Identifying the Stakeholders

Understanding who is affected by the problem or who plays a role in its existence and resolution lays the groundwork for a comprehensive perspective on the issue.

What: Clarifying the Issue

Articulating what the problem entails in specific terms helps to ensure that the team's efforts are precisely targeted.

Where: Locating the Problem in Context

Identifying where the problem occurs situates the issue within a specific operational or physical context, further refining the team's focus.

When: Determining Cadence

When trying to solve a problem, establishing the "when" can often provide critical insights into the nature of the issue, revealing patterns and circumstances that contribute to its occurrence. Understanding when a problem happens is key to determining its cadence and can often illuminate hidden variables or environmental conditions that might not be immediately obvious.

Why: Establishing the Importance

Addressing why the problem is significant to the organization or stakeholders underscores the urgency and relevance of the problem-solving effort.

With the answers to these foundational questions in hand, the next step is to distill the insights into a concise problem perception. This involves crafting a one to two-sentence statement that encapsulates the essence of the issue, informed by the agreed-upon responses to the Who, What, Where, and Why. Visualizing the problem-solving process as a funnel offers a vivid metaphor for understanding how the perception statement influences the journey from problem identification to root cause analysis. The top of the funnel, wide and encompassing, represents the initial understanding of the problem — broad, general, and inclusive of various perspectives. Here lies the perception statement, serving as the entry point for the problem-solving process. As the problem-solving process unfolds, particularly through the first five steps, the journey metaphorically descends through the funnel, narrowing the focus from broad perceptions to specific insights. Each step acts as a filter, refining the problem's understanding and gradually honing in on the most critical aspects that need addressing. Achieving consensus on the problem statement is a foundational step in any problem-solving event, setting the stage for a focused and cohesive effort.

SIPOC

Step 1 can often seem broad and overwhelming. However, it's important that this initial step is focused and as stated before it can also be broad and encompassing but not too broad and open-ended. One effective tool for practical problem-solving that achieves this focus is the SIPOC diagram, which stands for Supplier, Input, Process, Output, and Customer. By using the SIPOC tool, you can narrow your focus and enhance productivity, ensuring that your efforts are directed towards meaningful and actionable insights. Each element of SIPOC serves a distinct purpose:

- **Supplier (S)** refers to the entities that provide the necessary inputs for the process.

- **Input (I)** represents the resources, information, or materials required to execute the process.

- **Process (P)** is the series of steps or activities that transform inputs into outputs.

- **Output (O)** denotes the products, services, or results produced by the process.

- **Customer (C)** identifies the recipients of the outputs, who could be internal or external stakeholders.

SIPOC is particularly useful for identifying stakeholders, aligning on the overall process, and crucially, identifying waste within processes. Within practical problem solving, this approach can be particularly effective when faced with broad, open Problem Description statements such as "our processes are difficult to navigate" or "our processes are inefficient." By conducting a SIPOC analysis, teams can pinpoint specific areas to narrow their focus, allowing for more detailed process mapping and targeted problem solving.

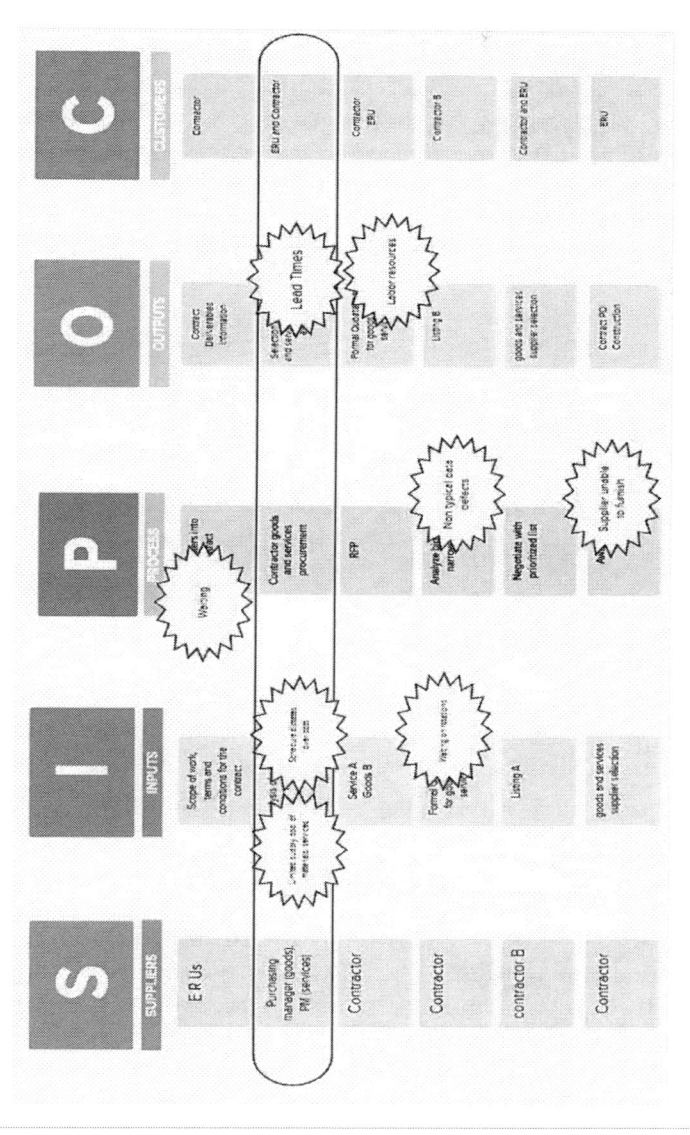

To create a SIPOC, start by defining the process steps horizontally, typically aiming for around six steps, though this can vary. Begin by capturing these steps vertically under the "P" column. Once the process steps are listed, work horizontally to specify the outputs for each step, the customers who receive these outputs, the inputs needed, and the suppliers of these inputs. Outputs should be specific, such as a data entry or an email, and the corresponding customer should be clearly identified. Similarly, inputs need to be precise, detailing specific data entries or work instructions. While completing the SIPOC, listen for feedback on problematic areas and mark these with Kaizen bursts or stars. This visual aid helps prioritize areas for detailed process mapping and further problem-solving efforts.

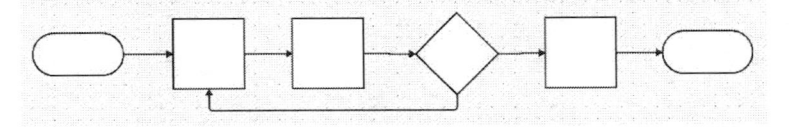

A process map, as mentioned above, is a visual representation of the steps involved in a process, detailing the sequence of actions and decisions required to complete the process from start to finish. It helps in understanding how a process works and identifies where improvements can be made. In creating a process map, each step in the process is depicted as a box, with arrows showing the flow from one step to the next. This can include inputs, outputs, decisions, and various paths the process can take. By visualizing the entire process, teams can identify bottlenecks, redundancies, or inefficiencies more easily. Once a problematic process step is identified through SIPOC, a process map allows for a deeper dive into that step, examining the specific actions and interactions that occur. This detailed analysis helps in finding the root cause of issues and developing effective solutions to enhance process efficiency.

After identifying and mapping the problematic areas, teams can address these issues one at a time, gradually improving the overall process. This iterative approach ensures continuous improvement and helps in creating more streamlined and effective processes.

Conclusion

Step 1: Perception, delves into the crucial phase of framing the problem accurately, which sets the groundwork for all subsequent problem-solving activities. This step emphasizes the importance of a comprehensive perception that encompasses who is affected, what the issue entails, where and when it occurs, and why it is critical to address. By organizing diverse viewpoints into a unified perception statement, the step highlights how essential clarity and consensus are beneficial to the problem-solving process. A well-crafted perception not only aligns team members but also ensures that the problem is articulated in a way that is understandable to all stakeholders, facilitating a focused approach to identifying and ultimately resolving the issue. As the team progresses through the problem-solving steps, this foundational perception serves as a guide, narrowing down from broad understanding to targeted analysis, ensuring that every effort is directed towards a meaningful resolution of the core issue.

CHAPTER 6
STEP 2: DEFINE OUR PROBLEM

After establishing a clear perception of the problem, the next critical step in the problem-solving process is to refine and define the problem with greater precision. This phase involves a deeper dive into the specifics of the issue at hand, leveraging data to transition from a broad understanding to a targeted focus. Data plays a pivotal role in this transition, serving as the bridge between the initial perception and a well-defined problem statement. By introducing concrete data, the problem-solving team can move from generalities to specifics, quantifying the issue and setting clear benchmarks for success.

Establishing the Ultimate Goal

The first step in defining the problem is to establish the ultimate goal, which represents the ideal state or the 'world-class' benchmark. While not always needed, this goal can serve as the north star for the problem-solving efforts, guiding the direction and scope of the intervention. In industrial settings, this might translate to achieving a certain operational lifespan for machinery or equipment, exemplified by the goal of extending the life expectancy of a felt on a machine to 120 days. This could also be 0 recordable incidents for safety.

Setting an Attainable Target

While the ultimate goal represents the ideal state, the target is a more immediate, attainable objective that serves as a milestone on the journey towards the ultimate goal. This target should be challenging yet achievable, providing a clear focus for the problem-solving efforts. For instance, setting a target life expectancy of 90 days for the felt, against the backdrop of an ultimate goal of 120 days, creates a focused and realistic aim for the team.

Analyzing Current Performance

A critical aspect of problem definition is assessing the current performance, which involves measuring the existing state against the established targets. This assessment uncovers the gap between the current reality and the desired outcomes, quantifying the magnitude of the problem and providing a baseline for measuring improvement. For example, if the current average life expectancy of the felt is 64 days, this data highlights the gap that needs to be addressed through problem-solving efforts.

Identifying the Performance Gap

The performance gap, calculated as the difference between the target performance and the actual performance, quantifies the challenge that the problem-solving team needs to tackle. This gap analysis is crucial for focusing the team's efforts and setting specific objectives for improvement. In the running example, the gap would be 26 days.

2. DEFINE OUR PROBLEM

Ultimate Goal: 120 days life expectancy of felt

Target: 90 days life expectancy

Actual: 64 days on average

Gap: 26 days averaged

Defining the problem with clarity and specificity is fundamental to effective problem solving. It ensures that the team's efforts are aligned, targeted, and measurable. Moreover, a well-defined problem statement, supported by concrete data, facilitates communication and collaboration, both within the team and with external stakeholders. In addition, Step 2 will become pivotal in completing Step 7 when you monitor for success.

The transition from the initial perception of the problem to a clearly defined and data-supported problem statement is a crucial phase in the problem-solving process. By establishing an ultimate goal, setting an attainable target, analyzing current performance, and identifying the performance gap, the team lays a solid foundation for targeted and effective problem-solving efforts. This precision and clarity in problem definition are essential for aligning the team's efforts, setting clear objectives, and ultimately driving meaningful and measurable improvements.

Conclusion

Step 2: Define Our Problem, deepens the team's understanding by incorporating specific data that quantifies the problem, bridging the gap between general awareness and targeted action. The process of defining the problem is meticulous, involving an analysis of current performance to establish a baseline, followed by identifying the performance gap that needs to be bridged. This clear, data-driven articulation of the problem not only ensures that the team's efforts are focused and directed but also enhances communication with stakeholders, providing a clear, shared vision of what success looks like. This step sets the stage for all subsequent actions, ensuring that each effort is aligned with the defined objectives, and forms the basis for monitoring success in later stages.

CHAPTER 7
STEP 3: BREAK DOWN OUR PROBLEM

In this LEAN journey through problem-solving, we have now traveled the initial stages of Preparation, Perception, and Problem Definition. This chapter shines a light on the process of dissecting knotty issues into much more manageable pieces by breaking down our problem. In manufacturing settings, this could be a rather easy step, but in transactional settings or environments that are not plentiful with data, this could be the hardest step to overcome. When there is a lack of data, it is important to get that data and it is important to acknowledge that getting that data may be painful. The effort will almost always be worth the impact.

Being confronted by complex problems is like being confronted by a whole pie. The idea is not that you would try to eat the pie as a whole but cut it into pieces that can be managed. This metaphor of slicing the problem encapsulates the nature of the problem breakdown technique by narrowing your focus into more manageable pieces. This way, the approach to problem-solving is easier, showing areas that need focus. You may hear things like, "there has to be a smoking gun" or "there is probably something simple that will solve for all our issues." I certainly have heard these and similar remarks repeatedly throughout the years. Here is my answer to those statements, rarely does tackling a giant problem ever amount to any tangible benefits. The problem is usually too large and too complicated, and the pathway ends up being heroism type brainstorming sessions that ultimately does little to solve the problem and likely only convolutes the processes already in place. The other even more valuable thing to note is that if there is a "smoking gun" that links a bunch of problems together, that means the Root Cause is common for those problems. You simply break the problem down and solve for the Root Cause and it will solve for all common problems. This means breaking down the problem into one slice and solving for that slice can ultimately solve for additional slices. This is something that happens frequently and therefore it is not necessary to tackle the whole pie and ultimately if there is a "smoking gun" for one or all of the additional slices, you'll solve for all of them anyways by simply tackling a single problem.

The structured tool in the form of a problem hierarchy tree or KPI tree is a useful and efficient breakdown. In this example, in the case of a productivity gap shown of

26 days, you can use the problem hierarchy tree to be able to break down the problem in a structured way. In this visual representation, relevant components of the problem with their interrelations become clear and allow you to trace a clearly determined pathway. Data constitutes the very lifeblood of problem-solving, by separating fact from fiction or *thoughts* of what is happening into *evidence* of what is really happening. Take, for exam-

3. BREAK DOWN OUR PROBLEM

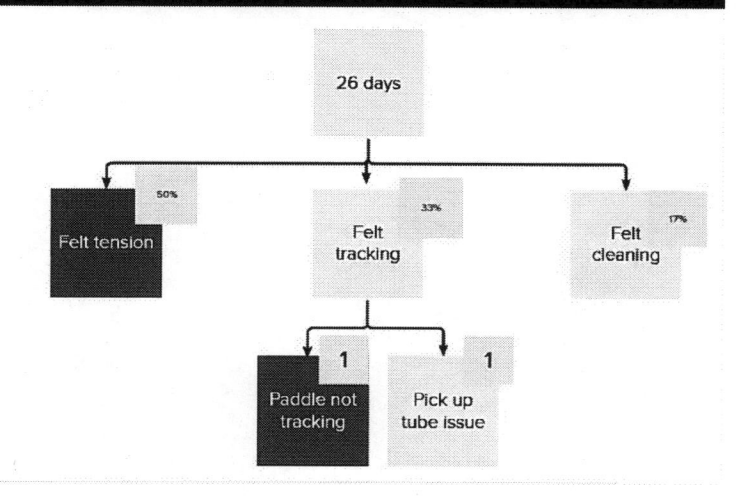

```
                    26 days
        ┌──────────────┼──────────────┐
       50%            33%            17%
   Felt tension    Felt          Felt
                   tracking      cleaning
                  ┌────┴────┐
                  1         1
              Paddle not  Pick up
              tracking    tube issue
```

ple, this 26-day gap where data analysis uncovers specific problem areas, like felt tension, tracking, and cleaning.

These major problems that are identified through data analysis: felt tension, tracking, and cleaning can at times be broken down further through additional insight into these problems by engaging with operators or those experiencing the problem through "Go and See."

Origin Problem Solving | Dustin Thomas

Prioritizing Problems

Now that the components of the problem are clearly spelled out, it then becomes a process of prioritization. Looking at the recent data in the example indicates that issues with felt tension have in-

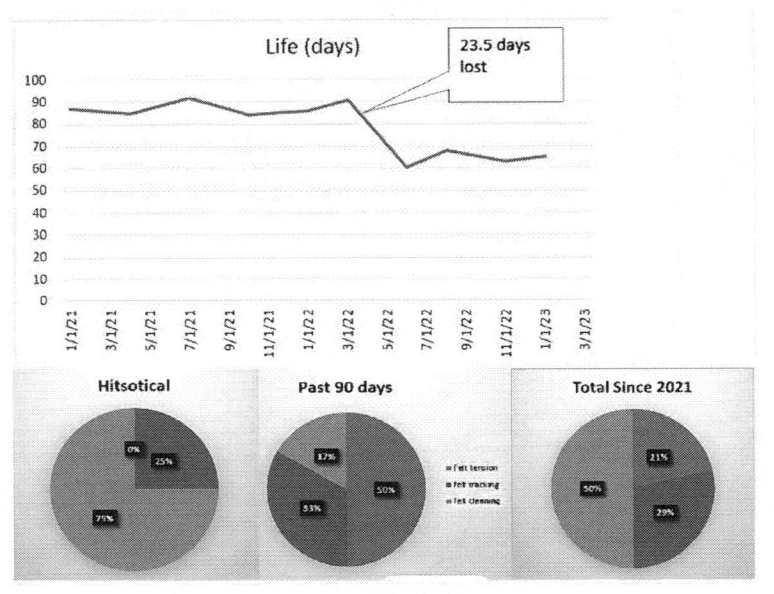

creased, and in this case, it would make sense to address these problems first. This is a decision based on things like effort (quick wins) or Impact (highest source of defects) on overall productivity the issue has. Almost always, a complex problem has more than one root cause and each of the individual problems needs to be solved. While looking at the problem list of tension, tracking, and cleaning, you should choose only one or two categories or subcategories to tackle.

Breaking down a problem is a critical skill in the LEAN toolkit. This helps the giant problems be reduced to manageable tasks, each with their very own solution and at times, common solution. This dismantling not only makes it possible to understand the problem at hand better, but also empowers teams to deal with each segment confidently and precisely. By breaking down the problems, organizations can better find their way through operational complexities, to finally get towards sustainable improvement and better performance.

Go and See

In Lean methodology lies a powerful practice known as "Go and See" or Going to the Gemba. This practice is rooted in the belief that to truly understand a problem, one must go directly to where the work happens—the Gemba.

Why Go to the Gemba?

Going to the Gemba is about seeing the actual situation for oneself, beyond reports and secondhand information. It's a commitment to understanding the reality of the work floor, identifying inefficiencies, and capturing opportunities for improvement firsthand.

Behaviors to Practice

Embarking on a Gemba walk requires a structured approach encompassing preparation, active observation, and follow-up actions:

1. **Preparation:**
    - Clearly define what you aim to accomplish.
    - Analyze the situation and collect necessary data.

2. **During the Observation:**
   - Compare the actual work with the standard processes.
   - Ask insightful questions to unearth underlying issues.
   - Distinguish between factual observations and theoretical explanations.

3. **After the Observation:**
   - Develop an action plan with clear ownership and timelines.
   - Address any unanswered questions and provide feedback to involved parties.

Key Questions for Gemba Walks

To gain deep insights during a Gemba walk, consider asking the following questions:
- How do you identify an exception?
   - Determining if the employee has a standard to identify a gap and by what methods issues are being resolved.
- How are exceptions visually represented?
   - Determine how exceptions correspond to visual management and are identified for problem solving.
- How do you input quality into the process?
   - Determining if there is a standard, the standard is being used, and if there are improvements that can be made to the standard.

- What problems do you have that you fix?
    - Determine what problems the employees see and how they are solving them.
- What problems do you have that you can't fix?
    - Determining what problems employees are seeing and how we are helping or enabling to solve them.
- What questions didn't I ask?

These questions help in understanding the standard operations, issue resolution pathways, and areas needing improvement.

A successful Gemba walk aligns with various problem-solving steps in Lean methodology, including defining the problem, checking progress, planning improvements, and ensuring standards are met. It's also an integral part of leader standard work, reinforcing the continuous pursuit of excellence. Embracing the Gemba spirit is more than just an observational walk; it's a philosophy that puts leaders in the heart of the action, enabling them to lead with empathy, insight, and an unwavering commitment to continuous improvement. By incorporating the Go See practice into the Lean problem-solving framework, organizations can foster a culture of openness, enhance operational efficiency, and drive meaningful change from the ground up.

When do I do a Gemba Walk?

- When Problem Solving step 2 Define Our Problem.
- When Problem Solving Point of Cause.

- When Problem Solving step 5 Analyze the Root Cause when necessary for validation.
- When Problem Solving step 7 Follow up.
- When in the Check or Planning phase in PDCA.
- As part of Leader Standard Work
- When analyzing Maturity Assessment progress.
- When determining a Standards review or assessment.
- Layered Process Audit to verify process adherence
- Waste Walk to identify waste

Conclusion

Step 3: Break Down Our Problem, navigates the essential process of deconstructing complex problems into more manageable segments, enabling a focused and detailed approach to problem-solving. This step emphasizes the significance of simplifying what initially appears as overwhelming challenges by breaking them down into smaller, actionable parts. Utilizing a problem hierarchy tree or KPI tree as structured tools, the step illustrates how to dissect a problem effectively, ensuring that each component is thoroughly analyzed and addressed. This breakdown not only clarifies the specific areas needing focus but also enhances the efficiency of the problem-solving process by isolating the most impactful issues. By prioritizing these issues based on their impact on overall productivity, the problem-solving team can allocate resources more effectively, ensuring that efforts are concentrated where they can achieve the maximum benefit.

CHAPTER 8
STEP 4: IDENTIFY AND LOCATE

Embarking on the next critical phase of Lean Problem Solving, we move forward with Identify and Locate. In this fourth step, we focus on pinpointing the exact location and nature of the issues at hand, thereby defining a clear trajectory for our problem-solving efforts. This stage emphasizes discerning the precise "where" and "what" - locating the problem within the workflow and formulating a well-defined objective for its resolution.

Crafting precise and achievable objectives by piercing through the maze of operational complexities utilizing the acronym SMART Target, helps us focus on that single slice of the pie that we identified in the previous step. This acronym stands for: Specific, Measurable, Achievable, Relevant, and Time-bound, providing a clear and quantifiable goal.

> **Specific**: Goals should be clear and specific, so you know exactly what you're working towards. This is why you broke down your problem in the last step.

Measurable: You must have criteria for measuring progress. If the goal is not measurable, it's not possible to know whether a team is making progress toward successful completion. Measurable goals answer the question of "How much?", "How many?" or "How will I know when it is accomplished?" You are using the data from 'Break Down Our Problem' to define your measurement.

Attainable: Goals must be realistic and attainable. The aim is to find the balance between setting a goal that is challenging but still possible to achieve. Goals should stretch your abilities but remain possible.

Relevant: The goal must align with your target and make progress towards your ultimate goal.

Time-bound: Every goal needs a target date, so that you have a deadline to focus on and something to work toward. This helps to prevent everyday tasks from taking priority over your longer-term goals. A time-bound goal is intended to establish a sense of urgency and prompt action.

For example, addressing a lifespan issue by aiming to achieve 90 days gives us a tangible benchmark. This goal is not arbitrary but is grounded in empirical data and feasibility.

In our scenario, we aim to bolster the lifespan to an average of 90 days and according to the data, this target is ambitious yet within reach. Setting a nine-month deadline is a balance between action and data collection but ultimately making it time-specific.

4. IDENTIFY AND LOCATE

What do you want to accomplish? Specific.	How will you know you have succeeded? Measurable	How can the goal be accomplished? Attainable.	Will the goal effect the Ultimate Goal? Relevant.	When will the goal be accomplished? Timely.
Achieve 90 days felt life on average	Track felt life	Historically the average life span of the felt is just under 90 days.	The goal improves the metric by achieving a target closer to the ultimate goal.	9 months

SMART TARGET
Achieve 90 days, on average, 2nd top felt life expectancy by 12/21/2023.

A SMART Target may not always be necessary, if your problem was already broken down when you began this journey and relatively few Root Causes exist, than your original Target, Actual, and Gap would be enough. However, if this is a complex problem, with multiple 'slices of pie' than a target specific to each issue is necessary to roll up to eliminating your gap.

Locate

With our Smart Target set, we move to pinpoint the 'Point of Cause' - the specific step in the process where the problem originates or is first noticed. This involves laying out the high-level process steps and scrutinizing each to locate the birthplace of the issue. If the problem's origin is ambiguous, we start at the step where the problem is first detected. The closer we get to the point of cause, the easier the root cause will be able to be uncovered in the next step. However, don't fret as tools in the next step will still be able to uncover the root cause with only a bit more effort if the origination step isn't specifically known. I'll explain more shortly. I want to make it clear that we are not solving for the problem, only indicating on a very simple process map, where in the process the issue identified is occurring or is first seen. This is the final refinement before we conduct our root cause analysis.

For our first issue, the Point of Cause was identified during the step of setting felt tension. For the second, it was during the lubrication of the paddle.

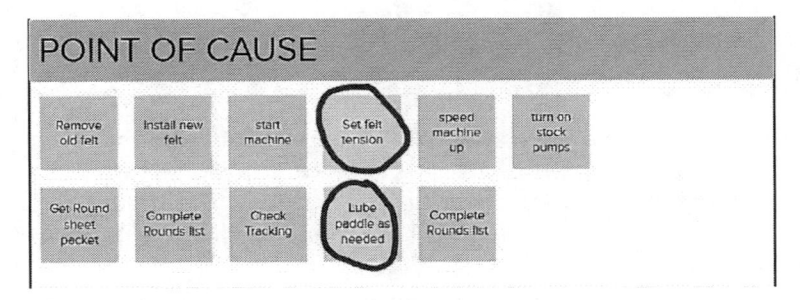

POINT OF CAUSE

Remove old felt	Install new felt	start machine	**Set felt tension**	speed machine up	turn on stock pumps
Get Round sheet packet	Complete Rounds list	Check Tracking	**Lube paddle as needed**	Complete Rounds list	

One story that helps illustrate the importance of identifying the point of cause is a problem-solving event that revolved around a hazardous and slick rock pile edge, which resulted in a sprained ankle.

It was early in the morning, and construction was about to begin on a vast expanse of land. Equipment was in place, and crews were on site. The project manager called for a huddle to start the day, and as everyone grouped together, he began with a safety tailboard. The huddle then progressed to discussing the day's events when an engineer received a radio call. To avoid disturbing the morning planning session, the engineer stepped back away from the huddle while answering the call. In doing so, they inadvertently stepped backward onto a rock ledge that was slick with morning dew, causing them to tumble and severely twist their ankle.

Origin Problem Solving | Dustin Thomas

I received the problem-solving report as part of an ongoing safety problem-solving review program. Upon reviewing the work, I noticed that the point of cause had not been utilized. The team had identified the issue but had jumped directly to addressing radio usage. From there, they proposed countermeasures such as setting up perimeters for radio use on construction sites. While some elements of their solution were decent ideas, I was not satisfied with the omission of the point of cause analysis.

To address this, I gathered the team back together and we started right at the point of cause, listing out a brief sequence of events. I then challenged them not to jump to solutions but to determine, within the simple process map, where the problem originated. After some discussion, it was determined that the problem originated at the safety tailboard. The purpose of the safety tailboard is to identify safety issues, yet the rock ledge hazard had not been effectively mitigated.

We then obtained the safety tailboard from that huddle and noticed that the rock ledge was indeed noted as a hazard, with the rocks identified as slippery. As we proceeded through problem-solving and into root cause analysis, we determined that the tailboard did not initiate corrective actions for the safety issues found; it only directed the team to identify hazards.

The outcomes of this problem-solving event were much more targeted and impactful. We incorporated simple standard changes to the tailboard form, resulting in significantly better risk mitigation. By focusing on the point of cause, we were able to implement solutions that addressed the root of the problem, rather than just the symptoms, ultimately creating a safer work environment

Conclusion

Step 4: Identify and Locate, advances the Lean Problem Solving process through the effective use of the SMART Target criteria—Specific, Measurable, Attainable, Relevant, and Time-bound—this step refines the problem-solving journey by setting quantifiable and achievable goals. This step not only clarifies what needs to be addressed but also where the focus should be within the workflow by identifying the point of cause. This step sets the stage for thorough root cause analysis in the following steps, and paves the way for targeted, effective resolutions.

CHAPTER 9
STEP 5: ROOT CAUSE ANALYSIS

Having identified and located the problem areas, we now dive into the heart of Lean Problem Solving - the Root Cause Analysis.

The Five Whys Technique

One of the most easily completed yet very effective tools at our disposal is the 'Five Whys' method. This technique involves asking "Why?" repeatedly until we uncover the root cause. It's important to note that the number five is not set in stone; the actual number of 'Whys' can vary based on the complexity of the problem, including how well the problem was broken down and how close we were to the Point Of Cause.

We begin the 5 Why by selecting the targeted problem from step 3 and then adding the location from the Point of Cause. For our felt tension issue, we begin with "felt tension too high" and then add the location as being setting the tension after startup. We then ask "Why" as many times as it

Origin Problem Solving | Dustin Thomas

takes to get to the Root Cause. To ensure the logical integrity of our analysis, we employ the 'Therefore Test'. This involves retracing our steps in the opposite direction to check if each 'Why' leads naturally to the next. If the sequence holds, we've found a plausible root cause.

Let's revisit our example. For the felt tension issue, the absence of a tension gauge led to subjective

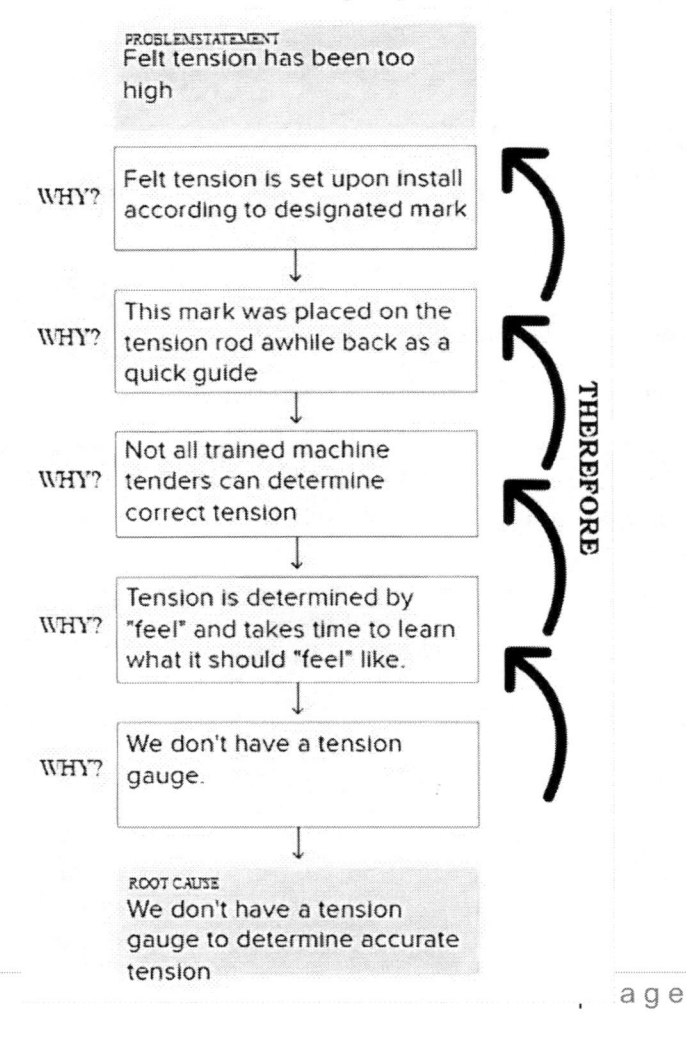

PROBLEM STATEMENT
Felt tension has been too high

WHY? — Felt tension is set upon install according to designated mark

WHY? — This mark was placed on the tension rod awhile back as a quick guide

WHY? — Not all trained machine tenders can determine correct tension

WHY? — Tension is determined by "feel" and takes time to learn what it should "feel" like.

WHY? — We don't have a tension gauge.

ROOT CAUSE
We don't have a tension gauge to determine accurate tension

THEREFORE

tension setting, causing the tension to be consistently too high. Through this analysis, we've not only identified but understood the underlying causes of our problems. To ensure our thought process is accurate, we start with the root cause and work back up saying "therefore" between each Why. If it makes sense then we are good, if not then do it again or revise your language. With these insights, we're now poised to develop targeted solutions that address these root causes, setting the stage for sustainable improvement.

Sometimes when completing a 5-Why, you will be faced with multiple answers to a single question. These answers will branch out, creating additional parallel lines of the 5-Why. This is called branching and is normal when there are multiple root causes. Typically, if a problem is broken down enough in step 3, you won't have many, if any branching. However, we sometimes just don't know what we don't know and arrive at the root cause analysis with several root causes. A few branches are okay but when there are too many, it can be very confusing and at that point you can either return to step 3 and work to break down the problem further or use other tools such as the Fishbone diagram.

It's worth noting that while the Five Whys is a powerful tool, it's not the only one in our arsenal. For more complex or less data-specific problems, techniques like the Fishbone Diagram or Kepner-Tregoe Problem Solving might be more appropriate. Experimentation is also an available and appropriate technique.

Kepner-Tregoe

While I won't go into detail about this technique, I do want to give you an idea of what a specialized process like KT can do and when the right time comes along, inspire you to research techniques like this in the future. The Kepner-Tregoe technique, developed by Charles H. Kepner and Benjamin B. Tregoe, is recognized for its structured and rigorous approach to problem-solving and decision-making, particularly in challenging business environments. It's most effective when dealing with complex problems where the root cause is difficult to determine.

Key Steps:

1. **Recognizing the Problem:** The first step involves the clear identification and articulation of the problem. This requires a precise definition that includes understanding the deviations from normal operations or expectations. Recognizing the problem accurately is critical as it sets the stage for all subsequent analysis and ensures that the team focuses on the correct issue without being sidetracked by symptoms rather than the actual problem.

2. **Finding the True Cause:** Once the problem is clearly defined, the next step is to drill down to its root cause. This involves a detailed analysis to differentiate between mere symptoms and the true underlying causes. The Kepner-Tregoe technique emphasizes data collection and factual analysis, urging problem solvers to look beyond the obvious and explore various dimensions of the problem, such as timing, geography, and process components affected.

3. **Selecting a Fix:** With a thorough understanding of the root cause, the third step is

selecting the most appropriate fix. This decision-making process evaluates potential solutions based on their feasibility, impact, cost, and alignment with organizational goals. The Kepner-Tregoe technique provides a framework for a systematic evaluation of possible actions, helping teams to weigh the benefits and risks of each option and choose a solution that offers the best balance.

4. **Avoiding Future Problems:** The final step in the Kepner-Tregoe technique focuses on preventative measures. It involves analyzing the selected solution to identify potential risks and implementing strategies to mitigate these risks. This proactive approach not only aims to solve the current problem but also ensures that the solution does not create new issues in the future and that similar problems are prevented.

Sound familiar? The technique integrates well right into practical problem solving and brings great techniques such as the "Is, Is Not" analytical tool that helps narrow down the actual cause of a problem by comparing what is known about the problem (Is) with what is not a characteristic of the problem (Is Not). This method helps in focusing the investigation, saving time and resources by eliminating less likely causes.

Fishbone Diagram

This diagram, resembling the skeleton of a fish, positions the central problem at its head, with various potential causes branching off like ribs from its spine. To commence, sketch or print a sizable Fishbone Diagram, ensuring clarity at the diagram's head where the problem under scrutiny is succinctly defined. The 'ribs' or major branches of the diagram should be labeled to categorize potential causes, traditionally segmented into Method, Machine, Manpower, Material, Measurement, and Mother Nature (environmental factors). These categories should be adapted to fit the specific problem at hand, ensuring all relevant areas are covered.

Employing ample space, such as a large whiteboard or plotter paper, is crucial to avoid overcrowding and to facilitate an open brainstorming environment. Ideas can be directly inscribed on the diagram or jotted on sticky notes for flexible categorization. As the session unfolds, encourage free-flowing contributions without rigid adherence to each category. The aim is to unearth a diverse range of causes, fostering a holistic understanding of the problem. Guide the team through the brainstorming session, elaborating on each category if necessary. If engagement wanes, refocusing on one category at a time can reignite discussions. The primary goal is to exhaustively explore different angles without being constrained by the structure of the diagram initially. After brainstorming, sift through the ideas, highlighting those beyond immediate control and pinpointing areas where data is lacking or could substantiate potential causes. With the diagram fleshed out, use the data to spark discussions, aiming to prioritize the most valuable contributors to the problem. Integrating the 5-Why Analysis at this juncture, with the individual issues, can further refine the understanding of the underlying cause.

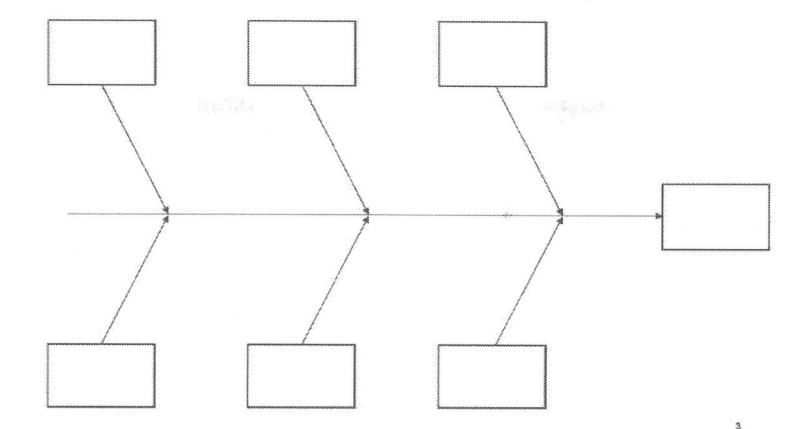

Conclusion

There are various analytical tools and techniques that are essential in identifying and understanding the underlying causes of problems. The Five Whys technique, effective for straightforward issues, involves iterative questioning to unveil the root cause. While the Fishbone Diagram helps map out potential causes across multiple factors, fostering comprehensive brainstorming and evaluation. For more intricate issues, utilizing more advanced techniques like the Kepner-Tregoe method provides a detailed analytical approach. These methodologies equip teams with the necessary insights to develop targeted solutions, ensuring sustainable improvements in processes.

CHAPTER 10
STEP 6: TAKE ACTION

Embarking on Step 6 of our Lean Problem Solving journey, where planning transitions into tangible action. Having traversed the path from problem identification to root cause analysis, it's time to confront our challenges head-on and implement solutions that promise real change. This chapter delves into the pragmatic facets of prioritizing and executing countermeasures to eradicate the root causes we've unveiled.

Prioritizing Countermeasures: Impact vs. Effort

The Impact vs. Effort Matrix is a vital tool, guiding us to classify our potential countermeasures based on the effort required and the impact anticipated. This matrix, with its x and y axis, categorizes initiatives into four quadrants:

1. **Quick Wins**: Situated in the upper left quadrant, these actions are low-hanging fruits with significant impact yet requiring minimal

effort. They are the "just do it" tasks that provide immediate benefits.

2. **Major Projects**: Positioned in the upper right, these initiatives promise high impact but demand considerable effort and resources. They are longer-term projects that necessitate careful planning and execution.

3. **Fill-ins**: Found in the lower left, these are the tasks we engage in when time permits. While they require little effort, their impact is also modest. Delegate these tasks when needed as "busy work."

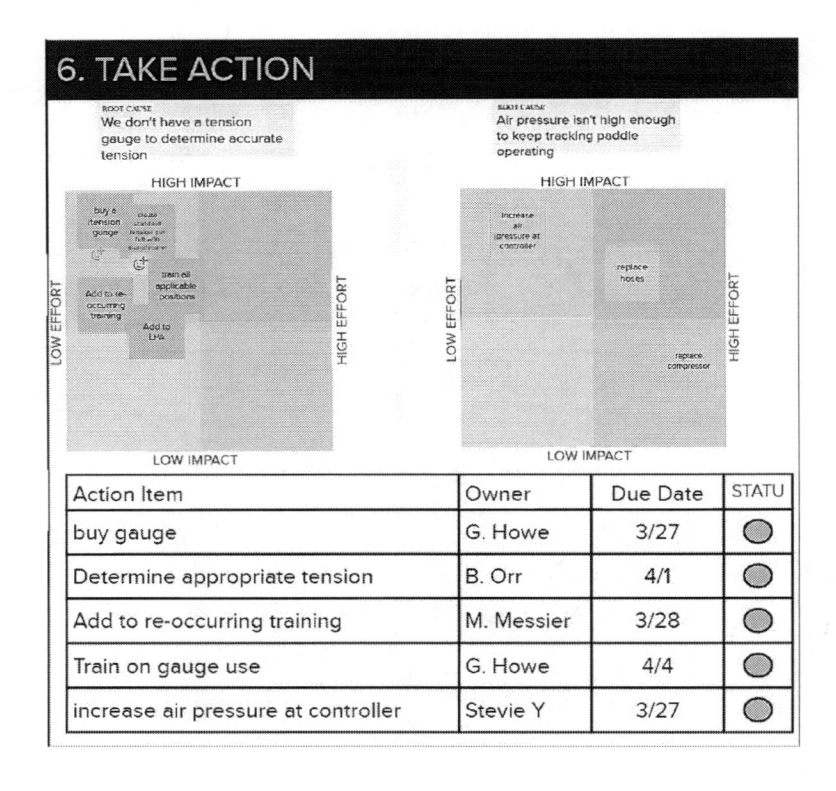

6. TAKE ACTION

ROOT CAUSE
We don't have a tension gauge to determine accurate tension

ROOT CAUSE
Air pressure isn't high enough to keep tracking paddle operating

Action Item	Owner	Due Date	STATU
buy gauge	G. Howe	3/27	○
Determine appropriate tension	B. Orr	4/1	○
Add to re-occurring training	M. Messier	3/28	○
Train on gauge use	G. Howe	4/4	○
increase air pressure at controller	Stevie Y	3/27	○

4. **Thankless Tasks**: Lurking in the lower right quadrant, these actions are both high in effort and low in impact, often deemed not worth pursuing.

The construction of an Impact vs. Effort Matrix should be a collaborative effort involving process owners, subject matter experts, and those directly impacted by potential countermeasures. The matrix should be sketched in a communal space, allowing for interactive discussion and estimation of both the effort and impact for each countermeasure. As discussions unfold and additional information emerges, the positioning of countermeasures on the matrix may be adjusted to reflect new insights. This iterative process ensures that the matrix remains an accurate reflection of the team's collective judgment. Following the exercise, the team should prioritize countermeasures as displayed on the Impact Vs Effort tool and an implementation plan for selected countermeasures is then developed, laying the groundwork for actionable steps towards process improvement.

Reflecting on our previous examples, we identified two distinct root causes: the absence of a tension gauge and insufficient air pressure for the tracking paddle. Applying the Impact vs. Effort Matrix, we generated a list of countermeasures:

- For the tension gauge issue, potential solutions like purchasing a tension gauge and standardized training for Machine Tenders were marked as quick wins—low in effort but high in potential impact.

- In contrast, for the air pressure issue, increasing the controller's air pressure was an immediate action, whereas replacing worn hoses or the entire compressor involved more effort and was categorized accordingly.

Detailed Action Plan

With our actions identified, the next step is meticulous tracking to ensure accountability and progress. A Detailed Action Plan, at its core, includes:

1. **Action Item**: The specific task to be accomplished.

2. **Owner**: A single individual responsible for the action's completion, avoiding the ambiguity of collective ownership. If everybody owns it, then nobody owns it.

3. **Due Date**: The target completion date, providing a clear timeline for action.

4. **Status**: A color-coded indicator of progress (Green for on track, Yellow for minor delays with a recovery plan, and Red for significant delays without a clear path forward).

For instance, the action item to purchase a tension gauge would be assigned to an individual (e.g., G. Howe), with a specific due date and a status indicator to reflect current progress. The owner is never a team or department, it is always a single person. Remember if *everyone* owns it then *nobody* owns it.

The journey from planning to implementation is rarely linear. Delays and unforeseen challenges are inevitable. When faced with setbacks, it's critical to reassess and adjust our plans. This may involve revising due dates or escalating issues to higher authorities for resolution. The key is to maintain momentum and adapt as necessary to keep moving forward. If due dates are greater than 30 days, look for ways to incorporate progress checks into your plan. What needs to be true at certain stage gates to ensure you are still on track?

Pilot

Conducting a Pilot can be a critical step serving as a preliminary test to validate the effectiveness of proposed enhancements or experiments. The primary aim of a Pilot is to verify the impact of these improvements and establish the optimal standard process in a controlled setting before a full-scale rollout. If existing standard work is in place, it should be amended to reflect the Pilot's requirements, delineating the specific start and end dates for this deviation. In cases where standard work is absent, the task is to develop it, ensuring it encompasses the Pilot's scope, duration, and participants. Training for the Pilot group is done to ensure adherence to the new process, as deviations could distort the Pilot's outcomes.

The primary aim of a Pilot is to verify the impact of these improvements and establish the optimal standard process in a controlled setting before a full-scale rollout.

A successful Pilot hinges on rigorous data collection that is accomplished in step 7 of practical problem solving. Baseline data from the problem-solving event is crucial to establish the current state, against which the Pilot's effectiveness can be measured. Continuous data collection throughout the Pilot, mirroring baseline methods, ensures the integrity of results. Additionally, monitoring metrics that might be adversely affected by the Pilot is essential to safeguard against unintended consequences. The Pilot's success is measured by its performance relative to the previous process, with improvements expected to be quantifiable and sustainable. If the Pilot yields positive results without detrimental side effects, it sets the stage for standardization and broader implementation.

Short term vs Long term

I spoke earlier about my thoughts on short-term countermeasures enacted prior to problem solving. At this juncture, it is yet again essential to talk further about short-term countermeasures and what long-term countermeasures look like.

Short-term countermeasures, such as one-off training sessions or initial messaging, are typically quick fixes that temporarily address issues but may not sustain over time due to their temporary nature. In contrast, long-term countermeasures aim to establish or enhance standards and are designed to provide lasting solutions. For instance, training can evolve into a long-term countermeasure if it's integrated into a recurring program or becomes an annual requirement. Similarly, long-term solutions often involve repairing or upgrading equipment, in addition to revising processes. When formulating action plans, it is vital to clearly identify whether each action is intended as a temporary fix or a sustainable solution, ensuring that every root cause is matched with at least one long-term countermeasure to guarantee comprehensive and enduring problem resolution.

Conclusion

Step 6, Take Action, encapsulates the transition from planning to execution in the Lean Problem-Solving journey, focusing on the practical aspects of implementing solutions that address identified root causes. Utilizing tools like the Impact vs. Effort Matrix, this step guides us through the process of prioritizing countermeasures effectively. This matrix helps distinguish between 'Quick Wins,' 'Major Projects,' 'Fill-ins,' and 'Thankless Tasks,' ensuring that teams focus their energies on interventions that offer the greatest benefits with manageable efforts. Following the prioritization, a detailed action plan is developed, which specifies action items, assigns ownership, sets deadlines, and tracks progress through status indicators. This systematic approach can be complemented by conducting a pilot to test the effectiveness of proposed solutions in a controlled environment, thus verifying their impact and refining the process before a full-scale rollout. This step also differentiates between short-term and long-term countermeasures, emphasizing the importance of establishing long-term solutions that standardize improvements and ensure sustainable progress. Overall, this step provides a comprehensive framework for moving to action, ensuring that problem-solving efforts lead to tangible and lasting improvements.

CHAPTER 11

STEP 7: MONITOR FOR EFFECTIVENESS

As we venture into Step 7 of our Lean Problem-Solving journey, our focus shifts towards validating the impact of our actions. This critical step ensures that the countermeasures we've implemented are not just temporary fixes but are genuinely enhanc-

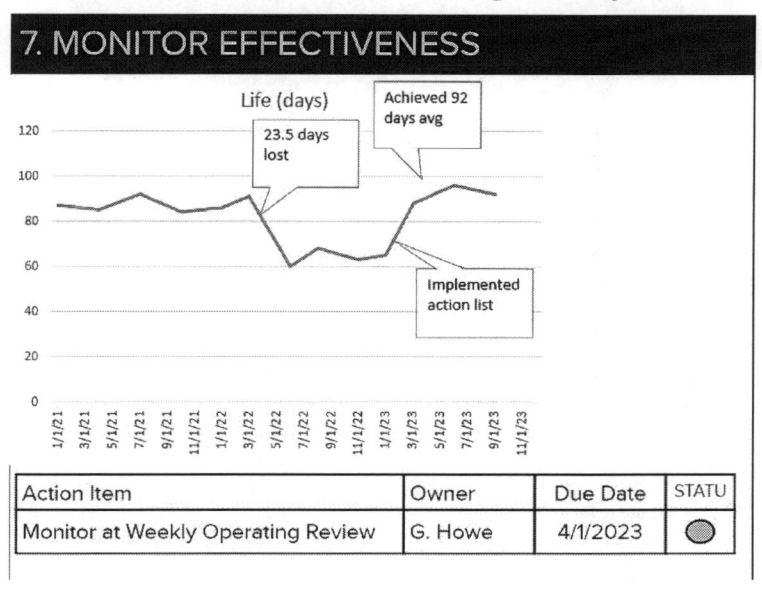

7. MONITOR EFFECTIVENESS

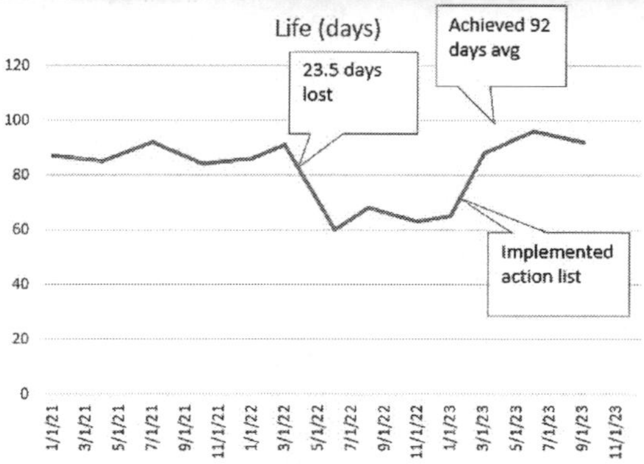

Action Item	Owner	Due Date	STATU
Monitor at Weekly Operating Review	G. Howe	4/1/2023	

ing performance and closing the gap identified in earlier stages. The essence of monitoring for effectiveness lies in the vigilant tracking of key performance indicators (KPIs) that were at the heart of our initial problem identification. It's about creating a feedback loop that continually assesses whether the changes made are yielding the desired results.

In our ongoing example regarding felt life expectancy, the responsibility of monitoring this crucial metric has been entrusted to an individual who will present findings in the weekly or monthly operational reviews. This structured approach ensures that the effectiveness of our countermeasures is not left to chance but is rigorously assessed through regular updates and analyses and that a focus is maintained even after all actions have been completed. The implementation of action items led to a noticeable improvement in felt life expectancy, from an average close to 90 days, with a dip due to issues, back to an average of 92 days post-intervention. This positive shift is a clear indication that the countermeasures are effectively addressing the identified gap.

However, the journey doesn't end with initial success. Continuous monitoring is key, as it not only confirms the effectiveness of current strategies but also highlights areas for further improvement, setting the stage for ongoing optimization efforts.

Financial Gains through Lean Improvements

Lean problem-solving methodologies aim not just at improving processes but also at realizing tangible financial benefits. To comprehend the financial implications of Lean initiatives, it's essential to start with the metrics that Lean efforts have improved. These metrics might range from reduced cycle times and defect rates to enhanced quality and delivery performance. Each improvement, when properly quantified, can be aligned with financial gains.

Key Steps to Quantifying Financial Gains

1. **Identify the Improvement Metrics:** Begin by pinpointing the specific Lean metrics that have been improved. For instance, reduction in safety incidents, decrease in defect rates, or reduction in cycle times. Clearly delineate the 'before' and 'after' states to showcase the improvement.

2. **Verification of Financial Impact:** Transitioning from operational improvements to financial gains involves collaboration with financial partners to obtain necessary cost/unit data, labor rates, and other relevant financial figures.

3. **Types of Savings:** Understanding the distinction between soft and hard savings is crucial:

    a) Hard Savings: These are direct savings reflected on the income statement, such as reduced costs or increased revenues.

    b) Soft Savings: These savings might not directly appear on financial statements but contribute to efficiency, such as time savings or process improvements that lead to cost avoidance.

4. **Verification and Monitoring:** Verifying the financial impact is crucial for substantiating claims of financial gains. Monthly checks against financial statements can confirm the continuity of the improvement and its reflection in financial performance.

The ability to calculate and communicate the financial gains from Lean improvements is pivotal for Lean practitioners.

Conclusion

Monitor for Effectiveness, emphasizes the critical role of ongoing assessment in the Lean Problem Solving process. This step involves the diligent monitoring of performance indicators to verify the impact of implemented countermeasures, ensuring they contribute effectively to closing the identified performance gaps. By assigning specific individuals to oversee the tracking and reporting of these metrics, such as the felt life expectancy in our example, organizations can maintain focus and ensure continuous evaluation of their actions' effectiveness. Furthermore, this step underscores the importance of not only achieving but also sustaining improvements. Continuous monitoring facilitates this by providing ongoing feedback, which is crucial for confirming the success of current strategies and identifying further areas for improvement. The step also explores the financial gains associated with Lean improvements, outlining steps to quantify these benefits, from identifying improved metrics to collaborating with financial partners to verify impacts. It highlights the need for a clear understanding of both hard and soft savings to articulate and leverage financial outcomes effectively. Overall, this step reinforces the need for a vigilant, structured approach to monitoring in ensuring that Lean initiatives deliver sustainable, financially beneficial results.

CHAPTER 12
STEP 8: STANDARDIZE SUCCESS

This step is about converting our fixes into permanent solutions, ensuring sustainability and preventing regression. Standardization involves embedding the successful countermeasures into the daily routines and operational checklists of the involved teams. In our scenario, the critical tension measurements that contributed to extending felt life expectancy are added to the machine tenders' and back tenders' daily round sheets. This inclusion guarantees that the new practices are not overlooked but become a regular part of the operational workflow.

STANDARDIZE SUCCESS

:tion Item	Owner	Due Date	STATL
dd tension to "rounds" sheet	G. Howe	12/15/23	◯
dd to LPA	G. Howe	12/17/23	◯

Included in this step is also to look across similar processes and determine if the actions done here can also be done in other areas. This is as easy as going back to Step 3 where the problem was broken down and reviewing with the team where countermeasures can be shared.

In addition to this, an essential component of standardizing success is reflective analysis. This involves reviewing what worked well, what didn't, and identifying areas for further improvement. Such an introspective look not only celebrates successes but also cultivates a culture of continuous improvement, where learning and adaptation are ongoing.

Layered Process Auditing (LPA)

To reinforce the standardization, we employ Layered Process Auditing (LPA). This method involves periodic checks by different levels of management to ensure compliance and consistency in the new practices. For instance, supervisors might, on a weekly basis, verify tension measurements recorded by the machine tenders, while managers might do so monthly. This layered approach not only ensures adherence but also fosters a deeper understanding and alignment among various team members, leading to a more cohesive and informed workforce.

Conclusion

Standardize Success, encapsulates the critical phase of transforming temporary fixes into enduring solutions within the Lean Problem-Solving framework. The focus of this step is on standardization, which involves integrating successful countermeasures into daily operational routines to ensure sustainability and prevent backsliding.

Moreover, this step discusses the importance of applying successful strategies across similar processes, revisiting earlier problem-solving steps to identify other areas where these improvements might be applicable.

The implementation of Layered Process Auditing (LPA) is presented as a method to reinforce standardization. With LPA, different management levels engage in periodic checks to confirm adherence to new practices, ensuring that these practices are consistently applied and understood across the team. This not only enhances compliance but also deepens the team's understanding and commitment to these changes, fostering a more unified and competent workforce. Overall, this step drives home the importance of solidifying improvements and leveraging them for broader organizational benefit, thus ensuring the long-term success of Lean initiatives.

FINAL THOUGHTS
ORIGIN PROBLEM SOLVING

As we conclude "Origin Problem Solving: The Lean Approach to Complex Problems," let us reflect on the transformative journey we've embarked on together. Lean is not just a toolkit; it's a mindset. The principles we've explored are more than methodologies—they are invitations to think deeply, act wisely, and improve continuously. It's about making a lasting impact, not just within the walls of our workplaces but in every area of our lives where efficiency and improvement are needed.

Remember, Lean is a continuous journey. Each step you take builds on the previous one, and every problem solved teaches a new lesson. The path does not end with the completion of a project; rather, it extends into every challenge and opportunity you encounter. Lean problem-solving has a ripple effect—it enhances your team's capabilities, boosts organizational efficiency, and can even influence industry standards. By embracing these principles, you lead by example, inspiring others to follow. Think too about the legacy you wish to leave. Whether it's transforming a struggling department into a model of efficiency or mentoring the next generation of Lean thinkers, your actions will speak volumes about the value of embracing change and seeking continuous improvement.

Now, armed with knowledge and inspired by success stories, take the initiative to drive change. Apply these Lean principles diligently and encourage those around you to join in this rewarding journey. Lead by example, demonstrate the benefits, and watch as the Lean philosophy transforms not just processes but people.

Reflecting on my own Lean journey, I am continually inspired by the dedication and creativity of those who embrace these principles. It's not just about solving problems; it's about discovering potential in places we least expect and achieving more than we thought possible. Lean has not only shaped my career but also my approach to life's challenges.

Together, let's continue to strive for excellence, innovate without fear, and forge paths toward a more efficient, safe, and empowered future.

To enjoy more content and an A3 example, feel free to visit my YouTube channel:

https://www.youtube.com/@ORIGINproblemsolving

Thank you for joining me on this journey. Let's keep moving forward, together.

About the Author

Dustin Thomas is a leading authority in operational excellence, distinguished by his deep expertise in LEAN methodologies. His career is notable for spearheading and leading efforts in the adoption of Lean Operating Systems in two key organizations, significantly improving their process efficiencies and operational results. Dustin's initiatives have been pivotal in driving a persistent culture of empowerment and continuous improvement.

A holder of multiple LEAN Certifications and an academic background in Engineering from Western Michigan University, Dustin is at the forefront of professional development, dedicating himself to the education and certification of employees in the principles of LEAN. His leadership in extensive LEAN deployments, which include the integration of Six Sigma and Toyota-inspired methodologies, has consistently delivered remarkable improvements, such as diminished operational waste and enhanced productivity.

Beyond his professional pursuits, Dustin holds God and his family life in the highest regard, viewing his role as a husband and father as his most cherished accomplishments.

Definitions

1. **5 Whys**:
    - The 5 Whys technique involves asking "why" multiple times to drill down to the root cause of a problem. It helps uncover underlying issues that contribute to surface-level symptoms.
2. **A3 Document**:
    - An A3 Document is a size of paper that provides a visual representation of the problem, analysis, and solutions, facilitating communication and understanding. It is a journey map or story board of your problem solving.
3. **Action Plan**:
    - An Action Plan outlines the steps, responsibilities, and timelines required to implement solutions and achieve the desired outcomes.
4. **Agenda**:
    - The Agenda is the blueprint of the event, mapping out discussions, breaks, and brainstorming sessions to ensure every crucial topic is addressed.
5. **Alignment**:
    - Alignment ensures that all team members and stakeholders have a shared understanding and commitment to the problem-solving process and objectives.
6. **Analysis**:
    - Analysis involves examining data and information to understand the problem and identify underlying patterns, causes, and potential solutions.
7. **Benchmarking**:
    - Benchmarking involves comparing processes, performance metrics, and practices against industry standards or best

practices to identify areas for improvement.
8. **Brainstorming**:
    - Brainstorming is a collaborative technique used to generate a wide range of ideas and solutions for a problem, encouraging creativity and free thinking.
9. **Breaking Down the Problem**:
    - Breaking down the problem involves dissecting it into manageable parts, focusing on segments with the most significant impact or easiest wins.
10. **Cause and Effect Diagram**:
    - A visual tool used to identify, explore, and display possible causes of a problem, helping to understand its root causes.
11. **Champion**:
    - A Champion is someone who may or may not be directly involved in the problem-solving event but is kept updated through Charter signing and report outs. They have the authority to push through countermeasures, especially in cross-functional situations, ensuring outcomes are adhered to and issues can be escalated for resolution. The Champion is typically positioned between the Owner and the Sponsor.
12. **Change Management**:
    - Change Management involves planning, implementing, and monitoring changes to ensure successful adoption and minimize resistance.
13. **Charter**:
    - A Charter is a formal agreement between the Owner and the Sponsor outlining what the problem-solving event will accomplish. It typically includes the purpose, scope, objectives, and participants of the event. The Charter serves as a ref-

erence throughout the problem-solving process.

14. **Check Sheet**:
    - A Check Sheet is a structured form used to collect and analyze data in a systematic way, helping to identify patterns and trends.

15. **Communication Plan**:
    - A Communication Plan outlines how information will be shared with stakeholders throughout the problem-solving process, ensuring transparency and engagement.

16. **Continuous Improvement**:
    - Continuous Improvement is the ongoing effort to enhance processes, products, and services. It is a key principle of Lean methodology, focusing on incremental changes for better efficiency and effectiveness.

17. **Continuous Monitoring**:
    - Continuous Monitoring involves regularly tracking key metrics and performance indicators to ensure ongoing effectiveness and identify areas for further improvement.

18. **Corrective Action**:
    - Corrective Action refers to measures taken to fix problems and prevent recurrence, addressing the root causes of issues.

19. **Countermeasure Plan**:
    - A Countermeasure Plan outlines the actions needed to address identified root causes. It includes details of what will be done, who will do it, and by when.

20. **Countermeasures**:
    - Countermeasures are actions taken to address the root causes identified during the analysis. They are planned and executed to eliminate or mitigate the problem.

21. **Critical Path**:
    - The Critical Path is the sequence of tasks that determine the minimum time needed to complete a project, highlighting dependencies and potential bottlenecks.
22. **Data Collection**:
    - Data Collection involves gathering relevant information and metrics to understand the problem and inform decision-making.
23. **Decision Matrix**:
    - A Decision Matrix is a tool used to evaluate and prioritize options based on specific criteria, helping to make informed choices.
24. **Define the Problem**:
    - Defining the problem involves setting targets, measuring current performance, and identifying the gap between the current state and the desired outcome.
25. **Deployment**:
    - Deployment refers to the process of implementing solutions and ensuring they are effectively integrated into existing processes.
26. **Document Control**:
    - Document Control involves managing the creation, review, approval, and distribution of documents to ensure accuracy and consistency.
27. **Effectiveness**:
    - Effectiveness measures how well a solution achieves its intended outcomes and addresses the problem.
28. **Efficiency**:
    - Efficiency refers to the ability to achieve desired outcomes with minimal waste of time, effort, or resources.

29. **Evaluation**:
    - Evaluation involves assessing the results of implemented solutions to determine their impact and effectiveness.
30. **Facilitation**:
    - Facilitation is the process of guiding a group through discussions, activities, and decision-making to achieve a specific goal.
31. **Facilitator**:
    - A Facilitator is someone who guides the team through the problem-solving process, keeping the discussion on track and providing insights on how to proceed. If there is no designated Facilitator, this role is completed by the Owner.
32. **Feedback Loops**:
    - Feedback Loops are mechanisms for regular evaluation and adaptation of improvement activities. They facilitate continuous learning and dynamic response to new challenges and opportunities.
33. **Fishbone Diagram**:
    - A Fishbone Diagram, also known as an Ishikawa or cause-and-effect diagram, is a visual tool used to identify potential causes of a problem across various categories.
34. **Follow-up**:
    - Follow-up involves outlining the next steps for implementation and accountability, ensuring that the ideas generated during the event lead to tangible actions and progress.
35. **Gemba**:
    - Gemba is a Japanese term meaning "the real place," referring to the actual location where work is done, and value is created.
36. **Gemba Walk**:
    - A Gemba Walk is an activity where leaders and managers visit the work area to observe processes, engage with employees,

and identify opportunities for improvement.

37. **Goal Setting**:
    - Goal Setting involves defining clear, specific, and achievable objectives to guide the problem-solving process.

38. **Ground Rules**:
    - Ground Rules set the stage for interactions during the event, fostering a space where ideas can flow freely, and respect is maintained.

39. **Histogram**:
    - A Histogram is a graphical representation of data distribution, showing the frequency of different values within a dataset.

40. **Impact vs. Effort Matrix**:
    - The Impact vs. Effort Matrix helps prioritize countermeasures by categorizing them based on their potential impact and the effort required for implementation.

41. **Implementation**:
    - Implementation is the process of executing planned actions and solutions to address the problem.

42. **Implementation Plan**:
    - The Implementation Plan outlines the steps, resources, and timeline needed to execute the countermeasures effectively.

43. **Kaizen**:
    - Kaizen is a Japanese term meaning "change for the better." It reflects a philosophy of continuous, incremental improvement and is a cornerstone of Lean practices.

44. **Kaizen Event**:
    - A Kaizen Event is a focused, short-term project aimed at improving a specific process or solving a problem, typically conducted over a few days.

45. **Kanban**:
    - Kanban is a visual management tool used to control workflow and improve efficiency by visualizing work in progress and limiting work-in-progress items.
46. **Lean**:
    - Lean is a methodology that focuses on maximizing value by eliminating waste and improving processes. It involves principles and practices aimed at enhancing efficiency and effectiveness.
47. **Methodology**:
    - Methodology refers to the strategies and techniques employed to dissect problems, spark creativity, and find solutions. Choosing the right approach is key to the problem-solving journey.
48. **Metrics**:
    - Metrics are quantitative measures used to assess performance, progress, and outcomes related to specific objectives.
49. **Milestones**:
    - Milestones are significant points or events in a project timeline that indicate progress and help track the completion of key activities.
50. **Mind Mapping**:
    - Mind Mapping is a visual technique used to organize information, ideas, and concepts around a central theme, helping to generate and structure ideas.
51. **Monitoring Effectiveness**:
    - Monitoring Effectiveness involves tracking the performance of implemented solutions to ensure they are achieving the desired results.
52. **Objectives**:
    - Objectives are concrete, achievable targets that align with the event's purpose, guiding every discussion and decision during the problem-solving process.

53. **Owner**:
    - The Owner is someone responsible for the problem-solving event and is fully engaged in the process. They lead the charge in preparing and executing the problem-solving efforts, ensuring that necessary data and resources are in place.
54. **Pareto Chart**:
    - A Pareto Chart is a bar graph that represents the frequency or impact of different problems, helping to identify the most significant issues based on the Pareto principle (80/20 rule).
55. **Participants**:
    - Participants are the individuals involved in the problem-solving event, including thinkers, doers, and decision-makers. Understanding their roles and responsibilities is crucial for the event's success.
56. **Perception**:
    - Perception is the lens through which the problem is viewed and understood. It involves defining who, what, where, when, and why the issue is significant, aligning all participants with a clear overview.
57. **Pilot Projects**:
    - Pilot Projects are small-scale implementations of solutions used to test their effectiveness before wider adoption. They help identify potential issues and refine approaches.
58. **Plan-Do-Check-Act (PDCA)**:
    - PDCA is a cyclical problem-solving method that involves planning an action, implementing it, checking its effectiveness, and acting on the results to continuously improve.
59. **Preparation**:
    - Preparation involves gathering data, forming a team, and planning the approach to ensure a successful problem-solving

event. It sets the stage for the subsequent steps.
60. **Prioritization**:
    - Prioritization involves ranking problems, tasks, or solutions based on their importance, impact, and urgency to focus efforts on the most critical areas.
61. **Problem Statement**:
    - A Problem Statement is a clear, concise description of the issue to be addressed, outlining its significance and impact.
62. **Process Improvement**:
    - Process Improvement involves analyzing and optimizing workflows, systems, and procedures to enhance efficiency and effectiveness.
63. **Process Map**:
    - A Process Map is a visual representation of the steps involved in a process. It helps understand how the process works and identifies areas for improvement.
64. **Purpose**:
    - The Purpose of an event spotlights the specific issue or challenge at hand, diving into the 'why' behind gathering everyone together. It is the driving force behind the event.
65. **Quality Control**:
    - Quality Control refers to the processes and activities used to ensure that products or services meet specified standards and requirements.
66. **RACI Matrix**:
    - A RACI Matrix is a tool used to define roles and responsibilities for tasks or decisions, categorizing individuals as Responsible, Accountable, Consulted, or Informed.
67. **Resources**:
    - Resources refer to the tools, information, and expertise needed to tackle the prob-

lem. Identifying and securing these resources is essential for effective problem-solving.

68. **Risk Assessment**:
    - Risk Assessment involves identifying, analyzing, and evaluating potential risks to minimize their impact on the problem-solving process.

69. **Root Cause**:
    - The Root Cause is the fundamental underlying issue that leads to a problem. Identifying and addressing the root cause is essential for effective problem-solving.

70. **Root Cause Analysis**:
    - Root Cause Analysis involves using tools like the 5 Whys or the Fishbone Diagram to uncover the underlying causes of the problem.

71. **Root Cause Identification**:
    - Root Cause Identification is the process of determining the fundamental reason for a problem, enabling effective corrective actions.

72. **Scope**:
    - The Scope defines what is included and excluded in the problem-solving process, helping to maintain focus on the main issue without getting sidetracked by unrelated matters.

73. **SIPOC Diagram**:
    - A SIPOC Diagram stands for Suppliers, Inputs, Process, Outputs, and Customers. It provides a high-level overview of a process, helping to understand its scope and key elements.

74. **SMART Targets**:
    - SMART Targets are Specific, Measurable, Achievable, Relevant, and Time-bound goals set to guide problem-solving efforts and ensure clear, focused objectives.

75. **Sponsor**:
    - The Sponsor is usually a manager or executive who authorizes the time and resources needed to solve the problem. They make agreements through the Charter on what outcomes will be achieved using these resources. The Sponsor is generally involved only in the Charter signing and the report-out process.
76. **Stakeholder Engagement**:
    - Stakeholder Engagement involves actively involving and communicating with individuals or groups affected by or involved in the problem-solving process to ensure their support and input.
77. **Standardization**:
    - Standardization involves documenting successful solutions and integrating them into regular processes to prevent recurrence and promote consistency.
78. **Team**:
    - The Team consists of individuals or experts within the process who experience the issue firsthand. They are process owners and doers, and problem-solving cannot be completed without their input and expertise.
79. **Value Stream Map**:
    - A Value Stream Map is a tool used to visualize the flow of materials and information required to bring a product or service to a customer. It highlights waste and areas for improvement.